TEN THOUSAND PLACES

REV. HAROLD BUCKLEY

KINTYRE PRESS
703 Kintyre Terrace
Palm Beach Gardens, FL 33418

The front and rear covers, as well as all the other graphics in this volume were carved, photographed or drawn by Rev. Harold Buckley.

This symbol indicates that the piece has been recorded by Rev. Buckley and is available by separate order.

Copyright © 2012 Harold Buckley
All rights reserved.

ISBN: 0615493076
ISBN-13: 978-0-615-49307-7
Library of Congress Control Number: 2011945750
Kintyre Press, Palm Beach Gardens, FL

DEDICATION

In any dedication my family must be included as the air and breath of whatever I have become, especially so with my sister Elizabeth...the best.

But in this particular case I am dedicating this work to **Msgr. Martin O'Dea,** my first and only pastor. Whatever there is of gentility, or compassion, charity, or openness to people as they are, came from him. Whatever there is of a believing giver, he gave me.

"I say more: the just man justices;
Keeps grace: That keeps all his goings graces;
Acts in God's eye what in God's eye he is -
Christ --- for Christ plays in **ten thousand places,**
Lovely in limbs, and lovely in eyes not his
To the Father through the features of men's faces."

G. M. Hopkins

ACKNOWLEDGMENTS

I am most grateful to Greg and Cathy Hammill, to Bernie and Dottie Kennedy, to Claire and John Foster, to David and Joyce Tressler, whose help in the opening stages of this publication was indispensable. It was altogether generous and affirming, and continues still. I am especially grateful to Ken and Cheri Reynolds, who so graciously urged the work from the beginning and then needed no urging to *do* the work of reading, typing, and preparing the steps of publication. It would be incomplete not to mention the affirmation and actual *urging* of the many friends who had read individual pieces, and always the encouragement of family, and especially the morning Mass faithful at the Cathedral of St. Ignatius of Loyola, in Palm Beach Gardens, Florida.

CONTENTS

	Acknowledgments	i
	Introduction	xv
1	Compassion	3
	Again I Hear Her Moaning	4
	On Reading About The Death Of Lisa	7
	A Clown Christ:	8
	At The Catholic Worker*	10
	An Old Man At The Catholic Worker	12
	The Child With The Ancient Face...	14
	To A Young Mother In A New Age...	16
	Talisman	17
	At The Suicide Of Anne Sexton	18
	A Certain Sadness	20
	Outside My Window...	22
2	War	25
	Prayer For A Boy I Taught, Killed In Viet Nam	27
	August, 1945	28
	A Death In Iraq:	29
	The Pain Of Honor	31
	Other Places	32
	M. I. A.	33
	Freedom	34
	Soldier	35
3	Love	37
	On Your Seventieth Birthday	38
	Often In Good Nights	39
	Celibacy	40
	The Garden Wall	41
	Old But Not Forgetful..	42

	The Lock Of Love	*43*
	Time's Defeat	*44*
	Love's Time	*45*
	A Father	*46*
	My Mother	*47*
	Unlatched And Waiting	*48*
	If I Had Set My Heart	*49*
	"I Do…"	*50*
	Love's Fierce Fire	*51*
	The Green Wood	*52*
	Old Lear	*53*
	Love Is Loneliness	*55*
	A Child's Tale	*57*
4	Loss	61
	After Wuthering Heights	*62*
	Of Dust And Dreams	*63*
	Without Faith	*64*
	Poverty	*65*
	Pain Has No Name	*66*
	Past Regained	*67*
	Count The Times	*68*
	To An Unloved Child	*69*
	After Dress-Rehearsal Of The "Caine."	*70*
	Feeling	*71*
	For Some Children At Play	*72*
	I Never Met The Man	*73*
	Unfeeling Time	*74*
	What Will Stop	*75*
	There Are Places Where….	*76*
	London/Derry	*77*
	Courage	*78*
	The Wounded Thrush	*79*
5	Nature	81
	The Hawk	*82*
	September	*83*

CONTENTS

	Sudden	*84*
	Vermont	*85*
	Skies	*86*
	Winter Wakening	*87*
	Standing In A Night's Snow	*88*
	Walking In Silence	*89*
	To A Rose In October	*90*
	The Sound Of Summer	*91*
	Impassive Stone	*92*
	The Barn Loomed	*93*
	Cape Cod	*94*
	Autumn	*95*
	A Night Cry	*96*
	A Web	*97*
	November Night At North Sea	*98*
	The Catskills	*100*
	Is The Light Always Warm...	*101*
	The Gulls	*102*
	New England	*103*
	The First Fall	*104*
	Fearful Notes	*105*
	Nature's Gift	*106*
	Crossing On The Ferry	*107*
	A Shadow Speaks	*108*
	Why We Like Flowers	*109*
6	Devotion	111
	The Sensuous Rose	*112*
	St. Peter	*113*
	8:30 Alchemy	*114*
	To My Own Angel	*115*
	After Night...	*116*
	Renewal	*117*
	Blind As The Rain	*118*
	What We Dream	*119*
	When Morning Comes	*120*
	Is He	*121*

The Name	*122*
Good Morning	*123*
Holy Week	*124*
Last Night	*125*
The Annunciation:	*126*
Transfiguration	*127*
Rosary After Mass	*128*
The Gift	*129*
The Magi: A Journey	*130*
Good Friday	*134*
More Than A Dream	*135*

7	Search	137
	The Wrong Side Of The Sky	*138*
	Songs I've Heard	*139*
	A Soul Speaks	*140*
	Reflection	*142*
	The Alchemists:	*143*
	When Quiet Comes	*144*
	Darkness	*145*
	Emptiness And Song	*146*
	Aching	*147*
	Silence	*148*
	"80"	*149*
	How Cider Lasts	*150*
	Light Without Shadow	*151*
	To My God Of Silence	*152*
	Morning…	*153*
	Among The Palms	*154*
	Won't You, My Dear	*156*
	Moistened Clay	*158*
	Innocence	*159*
	Questions 101	*160*

8	Spirit	161
	Silence	*162*
	Seeming Death	*164*

CONTENTS

	Death And Dreams	*166*
	A Certain Moment	*167*
	Silent Cay	*168*
	Hope	*169*
	Meaning?	*170*
	Inklings	*171*
	On The Port Jefferson Ferry:	*172*
	Mirror	*173*
	Brooks And Leaping	*174*
	Walking In The Snow	*175*
	Tears	*176*
	Tombstones	*177*
	English Iii	*178*
	When They Meet	*179*
	After Gertrud Von Le Fort:	*180*
	Dryness And Tears	*181*
	My Father	*183*
	Here Along The Rim	*184*
9	Artist	185
	To Vincent	*186*
	Pebbles And Teaching	*187*
	A Word	*188*
	After Peter's* Class….	*189*
	Day-Done And Dark	*190*
	Le Jongleur De Notre Dame	*191*
	The Park Bench	*192*
	Now The Light	*193*
	Loveatlast	*194*
	The Artist	*195*
	Events	*196*
	Summer Emptiness	*197*
10	People who knew jesus	199
	Mary Magdalene	*200*
	Simon Of Cyrene	*209*
	The Centurion	*212*

	Old Simeon	*218*
	Judas	*219*
	Peter On The Lake	*220*
	Bartimaeus	*222*
	John The Baptist	*225*
11	Appendix	235
	First Line Index	236
	Fr. Buckley's Voice Recording	240

INTRODUCTION

It is not deathless prose or soaring poetry, but it *is* that private view of a public world that W. H. Auden called poetry. It is the voice of someone who tried to listen, if not always hear the sounds of life around him and beyond him. It is that search for the music of what happens, and what we do because it happens, or what we did to make it happen.

I am a priest who spent most of his life teaching Literature and Drama at both the St. Pius X Preparatory Seminary in Uniondale, New York and the college Seminary of the Immaculate Conception in Douglaston, New York.

Over fifty years of priesthood have brought thousands of meetings with, even *dealing*s with, the often silent but ever present Jesus. We meet Him in history but most frequently it's in our own or other's hearts. He certainly walked among the students at Douglaston and Uniondale.

God gives us fewer, but longer lasting gifts, we call talents. We can recognize them by the things we love. Within the orbit of my priesthood I had four great loves: Teaching, Poetry, Theatre and Sculpture. Since being at the college I had the pleasure and privilege of directing straight plays and Broadway Musicals in a collaboration of delight with Father Charles Matonti. I shared the incarnational struggle and joy of taking the Playwright's words and giving them human voice. His words were usually wonderful; so were the voices and the hearts of the student actors and musicians who brought them to life. But theatre is the most ephemeral of the arts. For a director, the making of a play, the work, the rehearsals, the moments of discovery, the miracle of casting, are all the things that last. The thrilling moments of light, on a stage, before an audience, where young men and women bring the truth of some playwright's dream to life can only be experienced, not told about. But it is over when the lights go out and the set is struck. It is therefore too elusive to be caught for this little book.

I *can* talk about, and show you what I mean in poetry.

Poets give us their private view of our public world. It is one, not only filtered, but felt, lived through, in their fiercely vulnerable hearts. They *dream* in their words; they *live* in their words; but mostly, they *love* in their words.

We can meet them in their words. I say *meet* them merely, not make great judgments about them, or draw deep conclusions, any more than you should make judgments or draw deep conclusions about the people you ordinarily meet in the daily rounds of your life. Some you may like, some be fascinated by, some you immediately respect, others you are 'turned off' by; but you live at your peril if you think you *know them.* People are mysteries. They are betrayed by being sorted, named, and pigeonholed.

Theseus, in A MIDSUMMER NIGHT'S DREAM, includes poets in his list of three fascinating forms of madness: the lunatic, the lover and the poet. He says of the poet,

> *"the poet's eye in a fine frenzy rolling,*
> *Doth glance from heaven to earth,*
> *From earth to heaven.*
> *And as imagination bodies forth,*
> *The forms of things unknown, the poet's pen*
> *Turns them to shapes and gives to airy nothing*
> *A local habitation and a name."*

I do not agree with Theseus that their work is madness. I think it is their gift, their calling; it is the glory of what they do.

W. H. Auden, memorializing Yeats, seems to be calling the rest of us when he says:

> *"Follow poet, follow right*
> *To the bottom of the night,*
> *With your unconstraining voice*
> *Still persuade us to rejoice.*
>
> *With the farming of a verse*
> *Make a vineyard of the curse,*
> *Sing of human unsuccess*
> *In a rapture of distress;*
> *In the deserts of the heart*
> *Let the healing fountain start,*
> *In the prison of his days*
> *Teach the freeman how to praise."*

Auden saw the nobility in what he did. None of us can miss the beauty.

All of my life I have loved the *nobility* and the *beauty*, and now keep in my memory what I can still hold of it. It is my treasure. Some men collect rare coins or exotic stamps; I have always tried to collect the music of human thoughts or events expressed in the notes of beautiful words. They continue to sing in my mind.

INTRODUCTION

With my little voice, I walked always among, and listened to, the great voices of the great men of letters, those Poets who sang our little lives to tears or laughter. They saw our worth and so reminded us to hold high our hearts for we are a little less than the angels.

Having had the privilege of walking among the great voices, having heard what I have heard, having read what I have read, how should I presume to print my little words and show them to you. Again I think Hopkins said it best when he caught and understood the kingfisher's fire, and the ring of stones in his roundy well. He heard in his heart the *tucked string*, and understood the *hung bell's* peal. They were *flinging out their name*. And he knew it was right because *"Each mortal thing does one thing and the same."* We deal out that being that dwells in each one of us. Ultimately *"Crying What I do is me: for that I came."* Even little things can say we were here.

I have included a few short pieces about people in Scripture whose meeting with Jesus I found so moving.

Lastly, sculpture, not being at all like the fleeting nature of even the most intense moments of a play, stands patiently just where you left it when you put away the chisel or the clay. The sculpted piece may not have a voice, but it does speak. When perhaps in frustration, Michelangelo struck the knee of his just finished "Moses" and said, "Speak!", he may not have heard an audible reply, but the "Moses" has been more than eloquent to the awed millions who have seen him since. Leaving aside the miraculous, uniquely gifted hands of Michelangelo, there is the greatest joy and pleasure when ordinary men pick up the chisel or warm the clay to find and release a form that no one else has ever seen. Suzanna Langer calls sculpture: *virtual kinetic volume*. It is a material mass that has the semblance of life. For me there is always that unforgettable moment, while my hands are working, massing, and molding the clay towards s some hint of life, that it *looks* back at me. Then I sense I'm not really alone; from that point on I know I must respect what's *becoming* in my hands. It isn't some mask of life, something merely superficial; there is now an energy in the clay or the stone that seems to make it capable. It has a breath that my breath can feel, that my hands were aware of and my heart will remember.

Michelangelo's David still looks out, as it did when the Medici were a force in Florence, at every other city state in Italy, daring them to make whatever challenges their foolishness might conjure. The veins in his arms still pulse through that strong but almost tender body.

I had taken a sabbatical when we closed the college at the end of the eighties. I enrolled at the National Academy of Fine Arts in New York. A whole new way of seeing sculpture opened up to me. There was a new atmosphere, certainly a very different focus. The academy had some very fine artists on staff and some wonderful instruction in the classes. I was particularly happy with the approach of Peter Rubino. He had a way of showing you an approach without imposing it; a way of explaining that opened other doors and then showed his delight in watching you come in. I loved being there. The years since then have always brought with them new commissions to work on, more importantly, to feel the challenge of. I have included photos of a few of them.

HB

Opposite: St. Rocco Caring for Plague Victims:

 I had been asked to do a statue of St. Rocco for the Church of St. Rocco in Glen Cove, Long Island. It is usually done as a single figure, showing his wound on the thigh and the conch shell indicating he was a pilgrim. So I read up on him and found out that he was on his way to make a pilgrimage to Rome. But the boat sailing from Odessa, had landed with mostly dead aboard in Genoa. They were carrying the plague. It spread rapidly. St. Rocco was told by an angel to turn from his pilgrimage and go instead to help the plague victims. And so he did. But while ministering to the sick, he himself was struck down. He was now lying sick in an alley, too weak to move. But to his shock a dog came each day with a chunk of bread in his mouth. Then wondering where his dog was going each day with the bread, its master came, found Rocco and brought him home and nursed him back to health. I show the saint caring for today's victims of drugs and aids. Rocco is pointing to the front door of the church, bringing them to Jesus. It's what saints do.

COMPASSION

Again I Hear Her Moaning

Again I hear her moaning in the night,
   and wonder:
       against what shore her feebleness,
      magnified by pity,
         will crash...roll back.....
         and then in a rending hunger-for-hearing,
                  crash again.
Some place in her, 'knowing'
  has broke loose from the currents that feel:
Some little bridge of blood has broke,
   and all the green-garden of her thoughts,
   so oft bouqueted to light by iris
   and the gentle, light sweet curving of her lips,
   has gone to gray and left her eyes to terror.

I hear her moan beyond the touch of tenderness,
   beyond the voice that asks her: "where she hurts."
I hear a million other cells of silence,
                of unknowing screams
     cry through her throat.

I hear them, as once from ancient caves
   becoming sense cried out against its knowing,
   or as a war-ungotten mother wails,
   or wives who now no longer need to wait,
   or fathers, brothers, sons, all lopped of love.

In the breaking up of life, do all our cries
      come to such a pass
   in little nights - black breaches - between the light?

Or is there not Another light, wherein she moans,
   beyond this little dark, so long surprised by dawn?

COMPASSION

Oh Father, stride like the song that sings your striding.
Lift her,
        shush her moaning with Your breath
            and with Your tears.
      Mock our heli-pads of mercy,
and Father-full, full-fold her in Your heart's home.

                              For a woman dying of stroke
                              Nov. 1982, Mercy Hospital

Once, when they thought I had a heart attack, I was in ICU at Mercy Hospital and I could hear her crying.

On Reading About the Death of Lisa

    is it enough to be sorry?
    to butter sadness on your bread..?
    to stir grief twenty thoughtful turns
                            into your coffee,
    where it stains, just under your lip,
                          on the side of the cup.

then, at refill,
       one drop on the "Times."
    why does it always fall on the puzzle, so that
    some word of the review seeps through 24 down?
                you fold Afghanistan behind
                           the death of a little girl, who
made the mistake of being born
    to some body whose old scars still bled
                not in tears but RAGE,

       you wonder how
    what's little more than a sentence in the "Times"
becomes BIG THICK BLACK shouts of ink in that tabloid
                across the table.

    what IS the size of pain?
    mean or mad or even from cold,
    when she hit the floor,
        a little bit of beauty would cry no more.
    quiet is not always better than tears.

       and NO!
             sorrow is not enough.

                                        1988

A Clown Christ:

"What? After he takes my cloak, I'm supposed to give him my tunic also. Is he mad? Did He really say that?"

"He did, and if you think that's bad, try this: "If he slaps you on the cheek, you must then turn the other cheek."

Then a third man shouted, "He said, 'Sell what you have and then give to the poor.' Not me. If He wants to sell what he has, Fine.

Why should we give it to some lazy lout who doesn't want to work?

If you try to help them, they spend whatever you give them on stupid stuff, or worse, drink."

"That's nothing, He even said, 'Unless you eat my flesh and drink my blood you can't have life in you.' At least there, a lot of the people He was talking to said, 'This is crazy, and would follow Him no longer.' That Great Russian writer put it in his book It was in BROTHERS KARAMAZOV. Yeah, there is a dream sequence where the Grand Inquisitor faces Jesus and tells Him He was a fool not to give those people bread. That's what they wanted. Then they would have stayed with Him. It's true He was a fool. You know there was a French painter, who often painted Him as a clown."

"Hey, that's it! A clown! Anybody who tells you that you can't follow Him unless you take up a cross, has to be a clown!"

So they went off together, and when they found Jesus they held Him down and dressed Him in a harlequin's outfit. He let them. That wasn't half as painful as the night when others would throw a purple cloak over His shoulders, get Him a crown of thorns, stick a reed in His hand, spit in His face, then kneel in mock reverence to His True Kingship.

December, 2010

COMPASSION

*AT THE CATHOLIC WORKER**

                                                        You were brave
to let so much of life in. Your tearless eyes
Reflect the tundra in the glaciered valleys
of your heart.
                     Burnt or frozen in season,
Thawed to life by kindness or by love, then parched
And parched again...and in the very doors of love
Found dying, if not *death*; the heart
That pulsed with tender passion, pulsed also to *time*;
Its beat will beat itself to death.
There is a lyric in our loving, but the metrics
Of the message are that it passes.
                     You could have stayed behind the
Safety of your eyes...within the silent limits
Of your ears...selecting only those touches
That could not probe, and would not *leave* your heart
                     What heart of artichoke and fatted
Bullocks would do to your now swollen or shriveled gut,
A morning's mounting gift of sunrise
Has already done to your once hungry eyes
And mind...too much of light and perhaps truth, and saying *YES'*
Has left you pebbled and benumbed...
                     Yes, you were brave,
And are tenacious yet; the grip you have on that valise
Is old and has the energy of habit;
And a very tired will.
Old Man, O don't let it go!
Your holding it, holds so much of me....
Denies my fear the luxury of shame.
Just your sitting there accuses me to courage.
I thank you.

An old man I saw at Friendship House. There were no cameras allowed so I sketched him when writing this piece.

COMPASSION

An Old Man at the Catholic Worker

           With still some wild wonder where tears,
Long ago, were wont to be
His bent and leaning look hung like a weight
That pulled his age so forward and so down;
Then seemed to startle every effort he made to move.
Even the chair seemed tired,
Though he merely hung, boney and thin-buttocksed
On the unknowing edge of it.

         It was the dryness of the eyes
That had known, perhaps, too much of water,
That struck me.
              The time of tears was gone or past.
The color of his life had washed
To the weary grayness of his equally tired suit...
His days of vivid tapestry,
Unspooled from youthful dreams,
Were salt-spilled and salt-spoiled;
Threaded in the rain of life upon his sleeve.
Only in his mind or memory was there wetness now,
Where all the old sounds were: tears of laughter...
                                                      once,
Or joy, or those we only know in the ecstasy of loving.
         O someplace in him he remembers being held,
That touch that said he *was*.
Now he looks for it again, but inside only,
In the dimness and haze of what had been.
Outside he hears a sound, his body knows you're there...
He turns to you or only lifts his head and after
A moment's unseeing stare, the pupils spark to suddenness
As though some door had almost opened and *he* was really there,
A light...almost a smile...
But presently he goes back though his eyes have not
left you) to search again among the dusty things
That once had made him *him*.

COMPASSION

He shifts an old valise with tenderness,
In which he seems to carry life itself,
And leaves you holding the wildness and the wonder
Like an echo where he sat.

April, 1976

The Child With the Ancient Face...

                Blessed
Is the Child with withered cheeks,
The Child with the ancient face.
Blessed is he, whose weeks were years,
Whose days drained dry
In the draining out of tears,
The Child with the ancient face.

  I saw him standing in the midst
Of a baneful
         Bombful
             Tombful ruin,
Looking like a lamb, or like Christ
Before the balcony of empty tombs
Who said He was a liar; beyond being priced
They called Him liar; cast forth from wombs,
To call their Christ a liar.

  How expect we less of aping sons
Who raced the course of time to split with guns
The steeple and the spire;
To pierce His hands with bayonets
And nail His heart (with all regrets)
On the cross of their desire.

              VERONICA,
Come wipe the face of this younger Christ.
The flesh about his soul is rent.
They have split his night of dreams with lead,
And left the matter of the Child so dead...so very dead.
(Women of Jerusalem, this part of what He meant.)

COMPASSION

   You munitions-makers, you masters of great battle,
You have veiled his sight with tears,
And scarred the morning of his skies with fears;
You have made his heart a hearse,

But he will carry all his dead to bury in your head,
And have the gray folds of your brain
Be tombstones for the slain.

   You lords in the market of war,
Looters of life, how much more
You can make today, with prices so very high;
From thirty pieces of silver to millions
For the 'few' who die.
                              But
Remember this Child is *blessed,*
He is high among the blessed.
For while you sat and diced about the fate of all the nations
You forgot: *he is brother to our Christ*
Through endless generations.
O you will see that he is blessed,
                           though his greatness you defiled.
  For the day will come when you shall meet
The Father seeking for His Child.

                                          December, 1959

To a young mother in a new age...

    You breathe heavily
And feel the pressure of a coming life.
Inside,
           It breathes your breath,
          And pumps your blood.
Outside,
       The air is waiting,
But it still smells the smell
Of an August day in 1945.
           It carries a death.
The Pacific atoll that was later
                        Changed –
Whose natives yet cannot go home –
Hears the ticking in the sand,
           As do the great sea-turtle's genes
Innocent in their eggs.
A few voices try to tell us of
          Some terror waiting in the rain.

O while you gather yourself for Birth,
A world of workers make the
                     mushroom tools
  To stop his breath.
  WOMAN, for your womb
             Who will weep?

                    August, 1951

Talisman

be tender or be mute
when it comes to loving.
be brief where words are only words.
if tears do not press against your eyes
don't claim the leap of love.

tears are the talisman of truth.

we know that words unsinewed by
the stuff of tears
offend the longing eyes of love.
and
lovers bedimmed by need,
themselves bedew the arid sounds;
reach with the heart's wet hands
to hold and stroke to life
some desert of unsaying.

saliva is to words
what tears must be to truth:
one makes the saying possible,
the other simply says it's so.

                                        an afternoon in 1985

At The Suicide of Anne Sexton

    Anne, at the edge of terror
        (later she would fall –
          precipiced and pressed past reappearing)
    told me in her liquid eyes
        a strength beyond our canonized
            or even utter fear:
                theologically uncomforted
                or madly driven,
    she walked where rocks of thoughts gave way.
    she fell like history into a well
the whole of us or part of us has never known.
    she touched and fed the animal leap of life
                that is our children;
    she angled in her arms the basket – by other norms –
                A BASTARD.

    O all life is misconceived but somehow loved –
        brought forth.... but   held:
        wrapped in horror and in hope.
    she knew this basket sucked the nipples of her nothing,
                  and her all....

        all is only all,
        nothing is never nothing.
    ANNE, I thank you for the edge you shaped,
        and sense its pain
                and know its truth
        by your sheer fall,
            sheer:
    all clear and fragile.
        truth:
    that in your muted larynx floats.
      and in our calling
    comes the same from out our loins

COMPASSION

                    as from our dying throats.
                       Hearts and limbs,
                       grunt and groin
                      are desert-bound
                  unless some other sound
                                reach
and lift us to a loft past life,
        where bastards are embraced,
                and withered hearts, called whores
are held by a GOD
            who never said he cared for names;
       and in his breath
            held warm
           the sometimes looked-for
          but unforeseen,
        limp of life that's known as
              Death

A Certain Sadness

                There is a certain sadness
sometimes seen in doorways
                    or leaning on a wall
                    (as the elevator closes)
usually in goodbyes;
              not born so much of parting
but of the unfulfilled moments
                      that went before;
those looked-for moments
              that we comb our hair for and wash
and tell ourselves they'll fill the very need
that makes us look and hope and comb our hair.

      and then
      they come.

but with them comes a lonely aunt perhaps
who spreads her silence across the air
so that it sucks up even the little sound
that's left from all the promise
that private thoughts had fashioned
                      for private telling.
        or maybe a nurse comes.
or the impatient unvisited turns upon his loneliness
and makes your conversation in its very richness seem
                            cheap.

        but whatever
        it was,
it has robbed the air of fullness and of touch....

COMPASSION

We have been apart too long to be without such need,
                        and yet too short a time
to have the heart's hunger, the longing soul
not care about eyes or public light.

                        and so we stand the silence
and the ordinary phrase and all the casual words
that act as though this were just ANYplace;
                that act as though our eyes were water
and all the tonal telling
            had not been said.

        so
        sometimes seen in doorways
        or leaning against a wall
        usually in goodbyes
        (as the elevator closes)
            there IS a certain sadness.

Outside my window…

                He was a child,
Shining-eyed and wide with wonder,
But stooped in some crystal corner of the rain,
Because the grass was bent,
Because the wind was cracking
The huddled flowers
    And the night was running
In the branches of his tiny hours.

             "Child,
From your warm eyes, why
Do you watch so the bent and broken grass?
Could you in the wide stillness
Of your white room have heard it falling
Or felt the cracking flowers
And stooped to lift the tender things
                    That pass?"

              He did not rise
Nor lift his eyes but lowered
Deeper with the grass.
Then I, remembering past hurts
And the fragility of love,
Felt words move in me like winter
    Toward this unsummered spring:
"Stand and dry your eyes I said,
gather up your heart, Child, from the flowers,
your tears from the wet wind.
For love is but the warm embrace
Of inevitable farewell.
It is the fond, but sterile, painting
of the heart for the slow severing,
the hard but usual loss."

COMPASSION

        In this way through
The broken night I spoke.
This way he heard me in the breaking of
                The light.

        Then stood he up
But not straight.
        His eyes were dry
But narrow.
          His face,
Like dry bones had withered in the spell,
And I knew, *God Forgive me*,
That I had taught him well.

                November, 1959

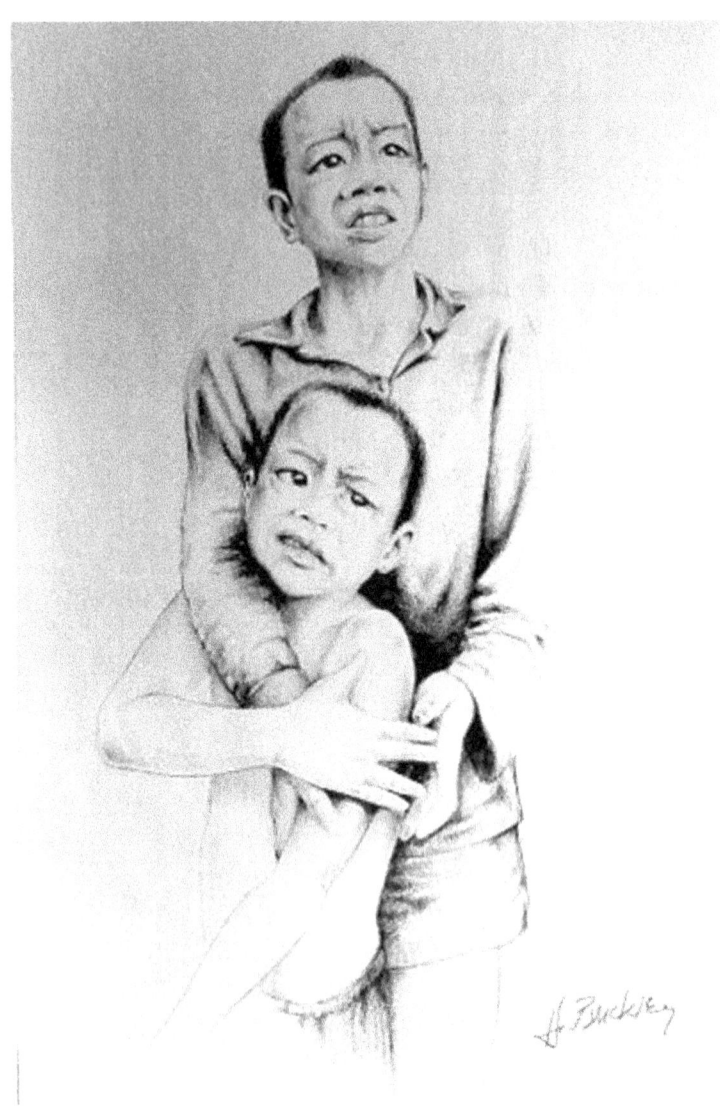

WAR

Prayer for a boy I taught, Killed in Viet Nam

Tears cannot unstop the silence made by shrapnel;
Nor light again his quiet eyes....nor yet unlock
      The laughter of his music days ungentled so
                          To sleep.
The deaf indifferent shells have made dumb
              The tender...probing lyric voice
Of his heaven-reaching heart.
And with their
      Weight of lead
Have bound him to the scarred and bleeding earth.
      For now the earth bleeds out in all his
                        Weeping wounds.
But time itself exploded in that steel,
      And all the boyish search for sound and light,
Beyond the reach of shrapnel and the
                    Cracking up of time,
Finds rest.

      He looks into the Face of Light,

And speaks the Word he sought in the turning of
Those
            Thousand steps,
Which led him to that slope of green,
Whose unknown name has now become so dear.

O Patrick, exchange the place I had with you,
      When by my role I walked ahead,
      And hinted at the sills of light,
          That you now *see*.
Hold out your hand and lead me home.

                                          May, 1968

August, 1945

    Prometheus is weeping by a rock
    In Hiroshima,
    Where there are no flowers
    Except the black ones the children drew
                              ......and were.
    From dying nipples
    They sucked a blistered milk,
                              And they died;
    Ovened in their mother's life.
                              And they died.
    Those whom the silence and the heat surprised
    Could not cry;
           But the fiery air was still humid,
 Tumid even, with tears.
I know the Titan is sorrier now he ever stole fire for us.
    But
                The rock was a cold thing
    Far from the petrified shadows of this sooted place.
                         And the rock, in its ice, said,

"Nagasaki."

A Death in Iraq:

He had that look, the empty, lonely,
            Futility-of-war look.
He tried to look at me,
            But there was nothing in his eyes.
Empty...emptier than skies
            Without a dawn....
                Or even a hope of dawn.
Without a cry, where the only word,
            Even among the stars, is *goodbye.*
Where are the other words? Are there any
            In the evensong of birds?
Will no one say, *peace....home.....soon*
            Tomorrow....?
Are the cries white?.....black?.....bearded?
                          or turbaned?
Is it Allah among the rocks?
            Or Jesus, where he bleeds?
Is it in caves or in front of friends
                That he weeps?
What dread voice sent him here?
            Is he dying for a mistake?

Oh, please God, not for a mistake.

Then he closed his eyes.

                                      August, 2005

Since the wars in Afghanistan and Iraq began, at the end of Jim Lehrer's Nightly News program, the pictures of men and women killed in battle would be shown in silence. With great respect he would say, "Here in silence are ten (whatever the number) more. We show them when their deaths become official and pictures become available."

The Pain of Honor

We see them each night:

Faces lopped of life, like flowers

cut from their stems, gathered and bouqueted for us

In a silence without drums, without taps.

Beautiful. But gone. Beguiling us with smiling faces

That can no longer smile, nor know our tears,

Or hear the laughter of all the love they might have had.

They reach, with their eyes,

For a future no longer on the other side of the lens

That holds them, indifferent and cold;

We long, as lovers do, to hold them in a warmth

That might have thawed the ice of that steel-jacketed

Hate which took them from our sight.

We watch, most of us, with a *distant* pain;

Not that of wives, or mothers, or fathers,

Or children who will never know the safety

Of a now only-remembered hero's arms; a hero

Who, now, might have been their 'mom', and now

They watch, through reddened eyes, their fathers cry.

March, 2006

Other Places

It was June.

Some men, with sand on their elbows,

Were testing the waters at Coney Island.

Others were dragging their sixty-pound packs

Up the already bloody sands of Omaha Beach.

A couple of boys were building a sand-castle

With a moat to hold off the ocean.

Their fathers were in that *other* sand,

Struggling to hold off death.

It was the same day, with the same sun,

Just different places.

July, 2006

M. I. A.

We are locked in what is *not*.

Something of what *was* still grows in us,

Not like moss,

Sometimes more like a scar, but always an itch.

The pressure of something partial,

Which *was* and *was not*,

Leaned its dark against us,

Which we named but never knew.

Now, we rue the loss, a past

Which holds more than what it told us.

Name, rank, and serial number

But never the *heart*.

All the tented, now rented, moments

With time's conscriptees are MIA.

The new heart's home opens

Old telegrams at the new door,

And reads: *"regrets to inform you...."*

Yet

Everything **will be**, and *was*,

Even in the dark that was our light.

March, 2008

Freedom

Waves came in like angry cockatoos,
Their crests all feathered foam and watery white.
The Higgins boats careened carelessly toward the beach.
Coxswains didn't know the men or any names huddled behind the
Remorseless ramps. Who knew which youth would change the color
Of the waiting sand on that indifferent beach?
No one seemed to know the *why* of so much blood,
Though some who sent them here had tried to gauge the cost.
No one knew.
                      God knew, but wouldn't stop their naked thrust for freedom.
God *couldn't* stop the gurgling cries in the surf that didn't care.
He read the bloodied cries for help soaking into the unsummered beach.
Why could He then, not stop the carnage?
Who *else* to rein in the dogs of war?
         He had made us free and would not traduce our freedom.
Jesus, with infinite pain and finite pity, must have admired the loving
sacrifice of men who poured out *their* hearts to keep their brothers free.
         He could not *make* us stop, without destroying freedom.
But to love, we have to be free to choose; even to choose the denial of love,
even to choose to hate. If we were not free to offer love, love would have no
value. It simply would not be love.
         There is a terror in the realization of how much He loves our freedom,
even how much He *respects* our freedom.

2010

Soldier

We waited,
    But no one came.
We wanted to call out,
    But never knew his name.
We saw his grave,
    But the poppies were all dead.
It wasn't ever
    What the poets said.
O the crosses did what they were told,
    Stood there white, indifferent, in the cold.
Our fathers promised we'd see the world.
    It was a lie.
Every lonely little town we saw,
    We just helped die.

February, 2010

LOVE

On Your Seventieth Birthday

Your lovely touch that tended brooding care
Was by care tendered, since hearts of beauty, bruised,
Are hearts more lovely; great from greatness used
Makes love from wearing-out itself more fair.

Your healing eyes that kissed the bruised wrong
Unlocked the light in childish darkness hid,
Made tall the word and set the dream to bid
Where ghosts and gifts and givers all belong.

The sun that watches your descent, ascends your son,
And turns the luster of your lovely light
Against the narrow, dark descending night.
Your course abridged, but 'twas beauty we saw run
In the waning of your light my light is fed;
And loveliness implanting love is never fled.

LOVE

Often in Good Nights

Often in good-nights
Lovers sway in place
Like some sweet music's metronome,
Afraid to stop
        Lest they end the lyric
           Or break some unheard magic time.
Their hands are hyphens in this silent song;
Their eyes a laser through the dim and the opaque;
Their cells unlock some longing too deep
                      For saying.
        And so they stand
        And sway in place,
And hold beyond the dark, in light-filled tears,
        Each other's mystery.

                                          October 12, 1983

Celibacy

though I have never held so sweet a holding
as then begets itself, nor let the ancient ache of warmth
have voice, to spill and fill the longing dark of love;
though sleep was ever and only sleep,

a silent willful dreamlessness (yet not undreamed);
though I have never shaped another's breath,
when in whose shaping my breath would come short
                                    or scarce at all;
still have I freed a thousand tongues
to get and tell their giving .....who later held *their* dark
to the different ways of light.
                                    And there are those
who held and hold my heart.....who somehow touch that cell-less
space which is most moved by never knowing motion.

How does my stillness speak? Is there in look or sound
some unseen silver bright coitus surprising
simple turnings with creation?
       Truly, meaning can be tender,
and tenderness be most in meaning.

June, 1985

The Garden Wall

Though I had seen the wall, and heard some call,
   Beyond the stones I saw.
   No flowers grew. For all I knew,
   The earth within was raw.
Have all such gardens no access
   And send but aromatic winds to bless?

I found a door, but nothing more;
   For all its bolts were drawn.
I stood outside, I wept, I cried,
   I begged the night for morn.
Does every heart play one small part, then watch the lights go dim?
   I wept and prayed the while I stayed;
But still I heard that haunting hymn.
   I tried to climb and then to crawl.
   I clawed the ground for yards around
Yet no one called, "Come in."

Is love so rare it cannot bear to have its flowers seen?
   Are buds so mute before their shoots
    Have bent the stems, in search of light, to green?
If love *will* not let you in, embrace the vagrant hearts without.
   Where leaner hearts that you will greet,
    Who'll ne'er outlast this endless street,
Will with their arms and warmth within, soon circle all your love about.

Remember then, *your* garden made, all nestled in your pastel shade,
   The pain you felt outside the wall,
    longing but to hear some call.
Unlock your doors, all open wide, to let a larger Love inside.

            June, 2004

Old But Not Forgetful..

The heart never knew that its sweet song,

In stranger's eyes could sound so wrong.

But here with many years of laughter shared,

Where suppers supped were ever bright

And stories lasted into night,

No tales of still remembered times were spared.

These later days from loss now shorn,

In truth, seemed youth was found again;

We smiled the smiles of happy men;

And grasped still tighter, the years we'd borne.

November, 2005.

The Lock of Love

Time, after all, has little hands.

They cannot pick the lock of love.

They may snatch up the droppings from love's table;

But two hearts, together, outweigh the worst of time.

Hold fast that fort with the exercise of trying;

When we are not in love, we are just busy, dying.

June, 2004

Time's Defeat

      Memory is the only faculty that can defeat Time.

              It can mock Time.

It reaches into Time's guts

                    And snatches its most precious moments.

Clocks may sneer at birth and even death

                    As passing.

It can laugh at the awe-filled tears of old people

                    who have forgot the pain of either.

      Even when the gift itself begins to fade,

It harks back ever to childhood

         To hold most clear and dear

The treasured days and acts of innocence.

        Memory is the hint that we are not ephemeral.

As it fades the images are warm and pure.

        We may throw our ashes to the wind.

            It does not.

                                                February, 2007

Love's Time

Though love be the dupe of Time,
Time, at last, will feel Love's pain
    When love itself shall pass,
But every love cut sadly short,
    (Once then thought dead,) will rise again.

For a Stranger walked Emmaus like,
    With Time that lonely path away,
Where some men thought that life was lost,
    Their light now taken from their day.

But love had only stepped *from* Time,
    To where Death can have no sway.

March, 2008

A Father

The Coffee was still warm.
                Resting on the corner of the table,
His thoughts were on the children.
       How great when they survive
       the need to serve themselves,
       and before they're old,
       let the love that loved them,
       enfold the arms their arms enfold.
He wanted them free,
      and knew that *giving* made them so.
He wanted them strong,
      and knew the challenge to give,
            gave their eyes that glow.
      that always there was "Yes" and never, "No."
He wanted them unafraid of risk,
      and smiled at how they dared to love.
He wanted them true,
      and heard the sinew in their voice.
He wanted them to face the dark,
      then in the day, rejoice.
He wanted them to dream,
      and saw their eyes on heaven.
He wanted them to lift their world,
      and knew their love was leaven.
He wanted their roots to reach quite deep,
      that their young hearts could safely leap.
He wanted love to show God's Face
      and talk with Him to be the base
Of wonder, and happiness; so thrive
      that they would laugh to be alive.
The wants he wanted, he never said,
      He hoped his life would speak instead.

My Mother

My prismed lady:
    a watery cast
        against the silence and the silhouettes.

I saw your day was slipping,
    in silver-misted hoar frost
    around your head.

I heard the memories of almost forgotten
    tears and years
    rush through the cataracts
        of your slowly drowning eyes.

Those memories of rock and sea and salt;
    seaweed "as a child" you said,
        "you popped in your fingers,
        and chewed the salt from,"
    distilling ancient oceans into your eyes.

How did you move those sea-shorn rocks
    into your feet,
    so that always you stood on stone?
How did you file the grass and the cow-belled fields
    into your heart,
    so that wherever you were was home?

You never need to go back
    when you carry the place with you.

                                June, 1992

Unlatched and Waiting

While a phono
        thundered the beat of bulls
      or ice cracked
in the shifting speech
       of cubes and words;
while verbal dice were bouncing
      down
        the green felt of inner ears,
I saw you pause and
          Look.
Behind your face was something
that could make me new.
   But you never said it.
In the wordless running of your eyes
I sat at earsill's edge
    unlatched.....and waiting...
But your silence closed my doors.

                1950

If I Had Set My Heart

if I had set my heart on hearts alone,
as children or as lovers do,
if I had turned my eyes
towards beauty of face alone or form,
and listened never to the
incense-bearing breath of mists,
or never turned in neighbor disbelief
at the ragged path of starfish on a shore,
nor felt the drowning of my seeking self
in bursting fragrance or in simple sound,
you might have mocked me then
as one who never knew the heart,
for having known too much of only hearts
alone.

"I do..."

You pick the locks of mystery with these so-little sounds.

You knock with them on Time's unbolted door.

the draught of love you taste wants now much more.

And so you come to pledge your "Yes" where love abounds.

You met a world away where Mary comes to walk.

And there, your eyes found hands to hold another's eyes.

You gathered love to keep where no love dies;

and with that Mother's care there is no need to talk.

Yet she will watch as Cana's sweetest guest,

And knowing that years can bring their share of pain,

She'll nurse your dearest seeds with her sweet rain,

And let her Son take care of all the rest.

So here, the first meal you share with all your friends

Is Bread unbought and Living Wine with love that never ends.

2010

Love's Fierce Fire

That pulse, dear heart, that binds us so together

Drives, besides our blood, the ticking death of day.

I feel from the sea, pounding past the heather,

Echoes which haunt my veins with rhythmic spray.

We long for the longest hour (yet feel it most alone).

Hands which hold our laughter still speed us to our end.

Wise men would hoard Time's wealth, and bemoan

Intemperance, the wanton way we spend.

I say lovers long for lovers and times apart seem death.

Twin hearts, we know, do more than double time;

For though embracing loves race faster than their breath,

And love's quick pace, becomes its own quick-lime;

Still when passion's wanting, Time merely lets us plod,

But struck by Love's fierce fire, we hear the clocks of God.

The Green Wood

Love is not a desert.

    It is the green wood.

It is an oasis among the silent dunes of time,

    Which *are* the desert.

And pain is the realization of mirage,

    It is that dryness after promise;

It is the fingering of a reflection while

    Reality is still aglow...but in the distance.

We, the exiles in this foreign land,

    In the desert of awayness and unrest,

    Are subject to such sad mirage.

Tremblingly we try

    To quench our deepest thirst

    By holding phantoms to our lips,

        And drink instead

An empty draught of shadows.

    May, 1948

Old Lear

Old Lear, in a court of his own making, poses one of the most self-centered of all questions. In fact, worse than that; it isn't a question. It's a demand: "Tell me how much each of you loves me. Then I will match your words with land. I will divide my kingdom among you; the greater share to the greater rush of words." For Regan and Goneril, there is a torrent, a positive superfluity of guileful protestations, which reach with a conjured and avaricious love, for lands far beyond the confines of Lear's little room. For he stands in the wretched robes of power, in a room just larger than his love, arrogantly doling out the only thing he ever possessed, his land, according to a measurement he never owned, love.

'Doling it,' meant he never really comprehended love. He will pay a bitter price discovering only one of his daughters knew the limits of love's lexicon; but even she trusted too stubbornly in those little words, which make our lives so large.

So too these workers never understood the gospel's word for wages. They think they *earn* God's love. They think He also doles it out. But, not so. Even if He wanted to, He couldn't. It would be against His nature. God IS love. On the reverse side of Christ's coin is kindness and gift. The 'workers' actually all received the same, because each one was filled to his own capacity. We hold what we can hold, at any given time. No more. All the rest He keeps for us, just waiting for our little hearts to grow, till they are deep enough and wide enough. Then the part we couldn't hold, with all the interest of His Love, is given. The 'workers' were looking for the wrong thing....even from the wrong point of view.

Jesus is saying His Father is not simply *just*; He is overwhelmingly kind and merciful....and forgiving. It is not mere metaphor that proclaims: *"Between the saddle and the ground, I mercy sought and mercy found."* The mercy is there because Jesus is there.

You don't earn God's love *because* you are good. You're probably good because of *God's love.* I think I hold *gratitude* a higher virtue than praise.

How wonderful that we are treasured so, that He should care so much for us....when so often we care so little for each other. When I reread this last clause, "we care so little for each other," I'm forced to hesitate. Certainly, there are in the language some truisms that bolster that view: "Man's cruelty to man".... "Man is the only species that kills its own kind." - which is of course patently not true - but you also see constantly, elderly couples in the supermarket still holding hands, or just going down the street, or all the young people in harms way, even as we speak. They are there for us, and for people they don't even know: men, women, fathers, mothers, sons, and daughters. Some have not even seen their own new babies, born after they left to serve their country. All that these soldiers, sailors, marines, airman, know is how much *they* miss their families, and try not to think about how much *they are missed.* There is so much love around us, so much right here in this room: Those with their families, those stroking their children or touching their spouses. I suppose the only thing I could say about that, besides being so moved by you all, is that you should know how much of the Holy Spirit is in your touch or your eyes; how much of *Jesus* is in that love and in your hands and in your eyes.

When His eyes light on your love *and on YOU,* He must say how right He was to take the scourging and the thorns, and every bit of weight **we** added to His Cross. That suffering was the way He opened the door to deeper love for us. It was how we were healed.

June, 2005

Love is Loneliness

If I said that "love was actually loneliness," wouldn't you all just give me that peculiar look, and think to yourselves, "O poor Harold, or poor Father. You know I think I could see it coming. Poor Guy."

But when you think about it: Love is bigger than any moment; it is even in its way bigger then life. But it can sometimes end in a moment; perhaps some horrifying discovery....whatever; or worse very slowly, when it oozes joy like a wound. And it almost *always* seems to end with the loss of one of the loving lives. But even there, we know it doesn't end, it merely changes. Emily Dickenson may speak of, *"the morning after death, sweeping up the heart and putting love away."* But we know that the love does NOT die with the body. As a matter of fact our hearts are frequently torn *because* it doesn't. So in what way could my statement be true? How could I defend it?

Love *is* loneliness; it is an *acting out* of a longing for communion....a longing for the Other; but even when there is communion, when there *is* another, doesn't some part of us remain untouched... remain alone? Certainly in embrace, any kind of aloneness is forgotten or squeezed out. But then, at last, we must turn away and pick up all the ordinary things that make up our ordinary life. *There* the process and the need for love goes on. We miss the other, and in the *missing*, the need grows stronger. Still it seems our hearts are bigger then our loves and larger even than our lives. It's not that the beloved is less; but, like Brutus' remark in "Caesar," it's that our hearts are more. Our human love is *all* that human love can be. It may be that it is more than we ever dreamed of, or hoped for; certainly more than we ever felt we had a right to. As in Les Miserable, we have loved another person and *seen the Face of God.* Nothing in life could be more than that. Yet there will come moments, in some crowded room perhaps, or walking along a beach, to the sounds of the waves, or some night when you've closed your eyes very happily, and yet you get that slight wisp of what we've come to call "ontological loneliness." A vague feeling of being alone, lost out here in the stars. Again, nothing or no*ONE* that we have loved, and in fact still love so deeply, is even the smallest bit less. It's more that there is this, almost unrecognized part of the heart, this infinitesimally tiny corner that somehow was left untouched. And I think it untouched, because it wasn't ours to give away. We come into life, as Wordsworth says, "trailing clouds of glory." And some bit of that cloud belongs to God. Only He can fill it, and only if we *ask*.

That untouched part of the heart can become a deeper love, the *deepest* love – when it discovers its longing reaches all the way to God; when it reaches not only outside *ourselves,* but to the source of ALL outside....to the source of ALL otherness.

It is the deepest, most mysterious part of us, where we often fear even to look....much less to stay. It is some space in the cells, in the imagination, in our very hope that always begins as empty and then through all our loves, gives some hint of fulfillment, some reverberating pulse, which is paradoxically, most fiercely *self* when it's reaching for Other.

I say we are afraid to stay or even look at that depth, to face *that* level of loneliness, love's mystery, because it may, in fact, be ultimately *unfillable*. We may be *terminally* void....alone with an emptiness that is incurable, absolute. We are terrified, in fact, that there can be no loving that is more than a moment. There may be the mushroom terror of no *Transcending Love*. Then Matthew Arnold in DOVER BEACH may be right:

> " *that the world which* **seems** *to lie before us*
> *Like a land of dreams, so various, so beautiful, so new,*
> *Hath really neither love nor light nor certitude, nor peace, nor help for pain*
> *....And we* **are** *here as on a darkling plain,*
> *Swept by confused alarms of struggle and fight,*
> *Where ignorant armies clash by night."*

Hopkins was, according to this, a fool, and couldn't ever have really felt any 'lion-limb' of God pressed against him, or his heart; nor in the morning, seen the *Holy Ghost at the brown brink eastward spring with warm* breast *and with ah! bright wings.*

Then indeed there would be no point in searching or reaching. There would be nothing worthy of the heart....only of the *senses*. There would be no essential difference between the mutual grooming of apes, the petting of dogs, a horse scratching its behind against a tree, and our delusion of communion.

But the very *depth* of our loneliness bespeaks so deep a need, so radical an incompleteness, so driving a hunger for the OTHER that it quite transcends the possibility of cells or the passing appetites of glands. Cells can create the signs and symbols that point out and accept the Other, but something deeper in us *longs* for the Other......some limitless capacity to embrace.....some *hunger* to embrace the limitless, **is *there***, that echoes the Image of the Divine. And it is there even if we are not....but especially when *we are* in love.

A Child's Tale

(Was this one of the children Jesus blessed...)

Like little children, we climb up on to the knee, slipping and scrambling to hold on; our Brother, always with a smile, gives us a hand, reaching down and pulling us by the arm or waist. We get onto the lap and grasping those heart-covering robes, we crawl up on His chest and get one arm around our Father's neck. I can feel my Brother's hand pushing my bottom into place; I want to hug my Father and then I feel that great, strong, gently warm arm enfold and hold me. It is the arm Whose finger sparked to life the soul of Adam. And being held like that I know He loves me, somehow more than stars, or planets, even whole constellations. I think I'll never forget this....but will I? Will any of us, because I'm not the *only* one there. How can He love us all? Yet I know He does and I'm not jealous. I am glad He does.

Then my Brother lifts me down. When I turn around I see this incredibly beautiful world, with mountains, some even have snow at the tops; and the sky has this most wonderful blue, just like parts of some of the seas; and there are these great sequoias and little mustard groves, with birds in them, and all those things running about. And look there, a garden. It belonged to Adam; I heard he had a lot of trouble there, but the rest of the world is so much bigger. Oh now I can see other people just like me. They made me think of my Brother and my Father, and I kept turning back to see if They were around. My Father and my Brother. Something in me really misses them; even though They made this whole world for us, even the stars and the quiet of the night...all for us. But now and then I still keep looking back. Seems odd.

I see all these people, beautiful, some funny looking, some young, old, tall and short, but as I turn from face to face, and the wonder of them, I keep looking for my Brother. He had something that I never see anyplace else. It was just like our Father. In fact, when I did see Him, He always talked about *His* Father. I say *His* Father because He seemed to know something about Him that we never knew, even when He tried so hard to tell us. My Brother's name is Jesus. I thought about Him so much, and His Father too. Now and again I'd get such a sense of missing them; almost like I was part of them. Certainly They were part of me.

Then one day I heard about this carpenter's Son, and *His* name was Jesus. There were all stories about how poor He was as a boy; and had to hide out in Egypt and then He came back. King Herod hated Him. He must have helped His father around the carpenter's shop, but mostly there were stories of how He confused the rabbis, even when He was just a boy. Then I heard He cured blind people, (that fellow at the pool by Siloe, remember him; well Jesus gave him back his sight.) He made the deaf, actually hear.....all that kind of thing. Still I wondered *why* He came here. He was so happy with His Father. Some rabbis said it was because of the mess Adam made with Eve in that Garden. They disobeyed the one thing God asked them not to do, a stupid tree and now it's a funny thing, you can't get into that Garden anymore.

But *I* think: **from the very beginning** the Father loved us so much that He was *always* going to send His Son, Jesus, to tell us just *that*: that His Father loved us so much He wanted us to share everything with Him. Even His Son. That we *needed* Him to make us totally happy. That's what He wanted more than anything and I think that's why I keep missing Him and looking back to maybe see Him. I have a very close friend who *did* see Him. He told me himself and I believe him. When you see Him, if you let Him, He'll really change you and make *your* happiness just a little more *special.* Jesus, when He goes, leaves enough of Himself that you have to love a lot.

I think it didn't have so much to do with Eden or Adam or even Eve. It was just that God wanted Jesus to come and tell us...and sadly even to *show* us. I heard Jesus a number of times and those men who followed close to Him. They called them Apostles. When ever *they spoke,* they told us about Jesus. Whenever Jesus spoke, He told us about His Father. THAT'S *why* Jesus came, **to tell us about His Father**. His Father wanted us to know how much we mean to Him. But we just didn't seem able to understand.

He told us over and over, He cured people for us; He made cripples walk and deaf people hear, and men who had never spoken, ran around shouting His name. Then one day He said, "There was no greater love than that a man lay down his life for a friend." We all stood there and nodded and said in our hearts that He was right. And a couple of days later He tried to make it even clearer; He said, "I now no longer call you servants or slaves. You are my friends. I am happy to call you friends." Something welled us within me when He said that. *I was His Friend.* I knew if I were His friend, then the Father must love me, (could it be?) the way He loves Jesus. But still we didn't understand. Maybe we felt too much like sinners and Somebody so good couldn't love sinners. So Jesus told us about this son who took everything he thought he had coming to him *from his Father,* went off to some strange country and made a complete mess of His life. He lost everything...ended up feeding pigs food even he didn't have. But all the while his Father was out looking for him, and when He saw him, He ran out and hugged him, and kissed him and put beautiful clothes on him and made a feast; because His son had come home. He didn't even let him say he was sorry. He already knew that and had already forgiven the boy, because the Father's forgiveness was the same size as His love. And how we thrilled to hear that story. He was talking about us. Some of us were crying.

Yet it wasn't enough. Nothing was ever enough. Washing our feet wasn't enough. Healing and curing and lifting us up till we finally believed we had some worth......none of it was enough. O, we nodded and marveled and even followed, some at a distance, but we followed. But we never understood. He wasn't just straightening up the mess at Eden; from the very beginning He was going to send His Son to convince us of His LOVE.

Jesus finally *did* what He had *said* about dying for a friend, that there was no greater proof of love. For so long we thought it was because of that Eden thing, but I'm sure it was for Love; He always wanted us to love His Father....And if we did, we'd have to love each other, I guess again we missed the point. Whenever He talked, whatever He said or did was to bring us to love His Father Who so loved us. I'm sure that is what He meant when He spoke about doing His Father's will; to bring our hearts home to His Father. That is why we are so restless and never seem to get enough love. Our hearts were made for Him and His overwhelming love. So He opened His Hands and His Side to make roads to His Heart. When He said to Thomas, "Come and put your hand in my side," He wasn't just proving He was alive again, that He had done what He set out to do; it was so Thomas, **so ALL of us** could see how far His love would reach, how far He'd go, and then we'd be convinced of His love. The wounds were not simply credentials of life, but invitations to love. They were doors to enter into His Heart.

But this love had a special gift, *this* Passion and Death had a special fulfilling Grace. It was the Resurrection of Jesus. And this resurrection was given as a *promise to us*. "That where I am, you also may be." This final act of Jesus, is what the Father had planned for us **from the very beginning**. It didn't simply come because of sin. It comes from...... *it IS love. It is at the end ALL ABOUT LOVE.*

2004

LOSS

After Wuthering Heights

Yes, there are Heathcliffs,
who, like old Lear
wander this world of wet,
drowning in their thoughts,
in merciless thunder and that
most incomprehensible of follies:
re-living lost loves

well, I have walked his moors,
and known those moments by the rock.
I too believed the stories of
my abduction; and in my heart
I have felt that prince's blood.
I knew those heights, Wuthering
or withering, as mine.

Oh, there was terror in your turning,
the wind that bared those rocks
and made the moor, has also
blown your early words away: the music
and their heather-magic spell are gone.

How our hearts do make our bodies fools,
but bodies pay back dead loves with pain.
they flay that pitiable mass,
that mindless muscle in the chest,
till all its beating cells are mean.

when all the dreams and all the men
are dead, the wind will bend the heather still;
the rocks will hang indifferent o'er the sea,
where wildness, for an hour, once had been.

Of Dust and Dreams

Some place in this leering night
Where water flows in quivering pipes.
I hear it only as vibration
Hammocked here in the candied seeming
Of dust and dreams, of dust *in* dreams;
Perhaps it pressed as rivers do
                            Quite damned....
            Whatever evil you have....
While
Ingrained the pressure loin-limbed to tears
The unseasoned spilling of eyes and man.

O will he drown in the white grains
Of fancy and April's cruel rains,
When the blind worm, dead among the winding sheets
Stirs itself to...and dies in the staining arid dream.
            O make it run the sun
            O make it run the sun
    Still let me lie
  I am tumbled over roundy rim....
I am tumbled but cannot swim.
                      It IS A GHOST!

Call me....
I drown in the wind...
For the wind my nets were torn
                            from me.
    There are no shipyards in dark Galilee.

Without Faith

superior minds and

      great hearts, without faith,

find their refuge in art and poetry;

poets without faith

find their refuge in music;

      musicians without faith

are left, I think, to sounds.

        It would be the cruelest of jests

that Beethoven would never hear the great quartets he never heard.

time works so hard to stop our ears;

it can turn our freshest hopes to fears.

Poverty

I loved them all.
and told 'forevers' without a lie.
Yet I sold them all for....something;
with folded heart, like arms, I watched love die.

Is the heart so vain,
that like some dilettante,
only newness distracts from pain?

is the heart so small,
that love must elbow love,
like cuckoos, from the nest?

what's in breath
that a simple tender touching day
erases all the rest?
Was memory always in some foreign pay?
Is *my,* not me?

If my words are seeming searching small,
so is my heart.
so is the question......
so is my *all.*

Pain Has No Name

I did not *know* thy name

Before the willows bent,

Before the dark hearse came;

My voice could not lament

So sweet a passing, nor tears

Erase the tumbling laughter of your years.

Yet who will walk on my sad street,

Or stop outside my unlatched door

That will not make me listen for the feet

That I shall hear no more.

Past Regained

I don't remember Time, with such a kindness, spent,
As this hour's promise so suddenly bestowed.
Always its treasurers in moments only lent,
But here enriches me, with nothing dearer owed.

How many years it walked quite blindly on my heart;
How many times I tried to say, "forgive";
How many beats so pulsed our worlds apart,
Till silence, surprised by years, said "live."

Jesus must have knocked so many times;
Or played for me the clown with so sad mimes;
I looked for words when I was sorely proud;
Yet honest sorrow rarely speaks aloud.

O gentle sun, so torched with ill reputed fame,
You've brought Time back and gave me back his name.

2004

Count the Times

We will count the times,

And seek the times.

Who loved then more than ought.

Remember times,

That never needed counting....

Surprised-by, more than sought.

Yet in the Webster of the heart,

Without some scholar's date above,

Would they not now define

The very names of love?

1965

To an unloved child

in those first steps with open heart you walked away,
not knowing Love, Who lights the womb of night,
and being born illumines then the day,
pouring his undemanding gift through other's light.

But *'how'* and *'who'* and *'must deserve'*....and *'sin'*
were thorns upon an unthorned rose imposed,
                              with looks that chained.
"If you do this...*then* will our loves begin."
But oft, not done, the gift was left ungained.

The pain of 'earning' love began your flight.
You took no road, yet endless miles,
But staying close (not near) as close almost as night.
You sat alone, in hollow, haunting, smiles.

>   But even in deserts, where storms are sand, not sea;
>   Who walks upon the waters, will walk to thee.

1982

After Dress-Rehearsal of the "Caine."

Clay is kinder to my hands...and heart.
When unwombed from palms and fingers, that to
The wet fine sand gave sinewed seeming life,
In all the freshness of its presence and its form
The statue stands, and waits, returning light into
The eyes which rode the hands that gave it life.
Not so the motion and the sound we mounted
In this curtained magic light of seeming.

The music-words I often penned in pain
will hold their lyric life until I pick them up again.
Not so the dancing light upon the eye,
The fire-flashing heart-felt flint of voice
That strikes the footlight dark to tears or
Laughter, and blinds us with its comet trail of truth.

For the stage has its own life and time: Life that leaps
Quite free and strong from out director's hands.
The better he's been, the more he's loved it
The less it needs him now. It has the Maryk blew'
And having fought to live, it says: "Go on."
I never knew that I should miss the making and the
Meaning so.

1965

Feeling

When I was a child

    The crushing thought:

Even flowers die.

But with some intervening

    Tearful years the truth:

Especially flowers die.

Life at best is perilous.

    The beautiful are fragile.

The tender must bear the weight of touch.

The open, suffer the intrusion

    Of unobstructed, unselected, un*invited*

        Entrance.

Oh, what a rich but

    Heavy weight

Walks in the heart of any moments's

    Turning...

1988

For Some Children at Play

When all the grieving and congregating hearts

Turn in circles to the torn, no longer tender parts

Of lips, yet but a nanosecond wet with coffee or with smiles,

Whose laughing children, caught playing without fears

There, near father's knees now gone; no time for tears

When terror, once locked in childish darkness and in night,

Now seeks them out by day and finds them in the light.

Past pairs of purest eyes, past twins to birth and mirth's

Bright core, tiny hands let go of arms (their own) when earth's

Round sound explodes their play and makes their day a night.

No one sees the crying Christ pick up those hands and hearts and eyes;

Nor see Him hug their deeper lives with deeper love and cries,

Louder than His own Cross-crowned words, to awaken

The Father by Whom He must feel again so sore forsaken.

July, 2004

I Never Met the Man

I never met the man whose death I mourn.
I only know his light from eyes
              that shall never see his light again.
None shall ever, now, surprise
              the vital moments of his laughter.
But find the life that leapt to love it
              in the light that lights his brother.

I never knew how tall he was,
              or if his shoulders blocked the skies.
I can only guess his stature,
              from the reaching of his brother's eyes.

I never knew how much he loved,
              or what his road from heart to eyes.
But I can all that world of heartfelt wonder
              in his brother's love surmise.

He had worn with honor the cap of green-beret.
He had walked with honor, and in honor
              Now he lay.
I do not know to measure
              the cost of lives poured out in war;
I have no scale that says
              if this young life were full or no.

I only know there is a brother
              who wears his manhood with a glow.

                      March, 1964

(To a student who lost his brother in Viet Nam.)

Unfeeling Time

where once I feared the unseen force of time's

unfeeling hand against your inward form,

and like an anxious watchman, who climbs

the crags to warn against the silent-stealing storm,

I cried your unseen griefs within my heart.

For there - alone - the ravages are all foreseen.

Remembering other loveliness I'd seen depart,

I wept your autumn, with your sweet buds still green.

But slow-paced Time surprises even fear.

And when I looked to share love's freshening dew

I found your still unfolding petals sere.

Some quisling heart had found the heart of you.

    And now while slow time kills at its own pace,

    Your killing-time will Time itself outrace.

1978

What Will Stop

What will stop
            when you stop laughing?
Will there be tears
            when your eyes go dry?
What doors will close
            when you stop knocking?
Will any planets
            leave our sky?

Will only willows
            continue weeping?
Will flowers then
            forget the sun?
Will music fail
            with no time keeping?
Will planets and trolleys
            no longer run?

No. Nothing will stop that I can see.
The world will continue its merry way,
      Except for me.
No one, but Jesus, and weeping
      me.

June, 2006

There Are Places Where....

Always the wide-eyed boy walking
In the new street is destroyed.
Always the innocent with particular pain
Falls from the fist of his father Adam
And his brother Cain.

Always the light licks of his lids,
Till forth from his small room
He'll shield his eyes from our blinding ways.
Palms fixed against the suns of this land,
He'll breed night with his self-protecting hand.

Then through his white throat
Men's crooked cries can carve initials in his eyes.
O, I and all my kind will scratch with cryptic powers
Man's mark that mars and makes him ours.

January, 1962

LONDON/DERRY

hate had fallen like a tree
across this bleeding Irish road.
the hours gone were 'hurt,'
those to come limped empty of all hope.
blocked by barricades,
                        history is held at bay.
time's ticking hands, the other side of stones,
tug at the shrunk but torn and hating hearts.

caves and stones and drawing on the walls
                                  again appear.
humanity is held at bay;
and flowers falter out of fear.
anonymous cars shatter shops and innocence,
terrors, timed and packed in trunks:
    gape mouths,
    close tiny eyes, like mimosa in the night,
    and mute the music of becoming days.

O Time in tears,
        remorse despised, call out in ways that are still kind,
                to Forgiveness now in exile.

unhappy the land where Forgiveness has no home.
"Don't leave us here!" a voice cried out.
one voice among the thousands, who with stones and blood
        are learning how to hate.
            it is the old man's patrimony,
            and their gift.

Courage

What hand will I hold

    When the dark comes?

What will my lungs do,

    When there is no air?

I used to think the pain

    Was part of the price,

    Something that had to be paid.

I don't think so now.

    Pain is just part of the happiness.

    And happiness just part of the pain.

They both are, oddly enough, shapes of love.

I've heard they make up the *'deal.'*

    But *is* there any deal at call?

I suppose there are those who *can* say,

    "The deal is off. I don't want to play at all."

December, 2010

The Wounded Thrush

we had taken the willow path

that follows down along the lakeside;

we had chosen the place

where autumn wept when summer died.

I remember well your laughter

as you scraped the dried out leaves among the brush.

then suddenly you stopped

to hear the painful cry of a wounded thrush.

and there, among the dead

that summer left when she had fled this year,

a voice just smaller than a sigh

wept its mournful music in your over-anxious ear.

you caught it up with far more love than care;

you pressed it to your heart....but crushed it there.

I wept at the thought of all the dead you'd see depart;

and the dry, sad digging in your heart.

NATURE

The Hawk

        I went at mid-morning round the house
to drive the hornets with a spray,
and there beyond the eaves
                in soaring silhouettes
I saw the hawks.
I remember how hawks, lazy in the sky,
                like prowl cars
uncoop their powers in sudden shock
against the lark,
against the fragile moment of the lark.
    or
        how the feathered blur of sparrows,
in the face of claws
              and the talon-sweep of wings,
would flutter from the skies.

"Oh there is beauty in the brawn-winged arc
                    and roll -
your talon-terror tearing of the sky,
though you do not know the beauty
                or the
                    dying.
But earth-bound, in thought-flight only,
clay-caught and kept,
we know too well the lark-sound of life
                we have erased.

we know too well the doves
who cried against the night,
calling in their terror,
to tell us how that talon-motion
        echoes in our hearts.

                              Ellenville, 1978

September

I have watched so many leaves go sere and dry;

Wild fields fade out in colors without names;

cocoons, first bell-free butterflies, then flames,

and faces I held so dear grow old and die.

I've watched the sun's slow climb to height,

then clouds fall fondled in the day's demise;

And now I'll watch till that fierce reaching of my eyes

lets go its grasp and gives itself to night.

Sudden

        And of a sudden, even at my look,
'Twas like a rose betook itself to flight,
And bondless of its stem, left its leaves
Like leavings left and petal-winged
It pounced upon the air. There dipped it
And darted like some unknown thing blown
Past the traffic of our skies. High flew it,
And with fear I, through it, felt the flight.
O 'twas strange sir, to see the range and blur
Of such unfettered motion there before
My sight; how wings waved and weaved and slit the
Air with sweetest wounds. Never rending,
Never ending but always with a lovely again
It rode the rapids of airy streams and with
Half-arcs hurled sparks from the flint rays
                    Of the sun.
           Eyes and heart and hurl of me hung upon the
                    flight,
And wishes woke in me, spoke in me like flowered
                    breath,
Dealt sweetest death to a silence glad to die,
When such a perfumed song was spilt and petalled
Down upon our air.........

                                     September, 1949

Vermont

Once, I too was great,
And changed the course of streams (as children do).
I dammed the running rainfall by the
Canyon curb – before the drains
Gave back my wet and burly world
To pavement deserts and to city feet.
Or on a special summer's day
When we picnicked in the country,
With another friend of equal dream,
I tried some logs and stones against
The laughter and the leaping light
Of a real and running brook.
At times we won.
And then the rippling sound grew deeper
In the damming – until
At last the water found another way.
And then we'd laugh.

But now along the Hudson's crowded edge
I see that rivers have won over man
And gathered *him* like stones along
Their mouths and sides –
To dam him there.

Vermont, June, 1971

Skies

Are you so sure that lilacs listen?

Are you certain that the ferns won't frown?

In the rain when all lights glisten,

Will they in fact be-gem the town?

I have often *'seen it given down,'*

And some I know who hold it true,

That dawnings spring from brinks of brown

And weep their tears in beads of dew.

No trumpets sound; only birds

Announce the day that paints our eyes.

Who will come, and with wild words,

Unmask the hidden grace of skies?

November, 2007

NATURE

Winter Wakening

I see the old fig tree winter-wrapped,

Black-tarped ungainly like a drunken shadow,

Struggling unsteadily, too tired to stand smartly,

As once it did, a novice in November

When cowled and cinctured tightly top to toe,

It waited, confident from conquered winters past,

To face the unfeeling ice and the faithless sun.

Her figs dreamed on in the darkened warmth.

They trusted that some holy hands would

Cut away the dark, let them see again the earth,

And with fresh words, call them to birth.

March, 2009

Standing in a Night's Snow

        My road seems wrong against the night,
Like a luminescent ribbon
                    Without light.
The ashes of this slowly dying day
                Should
                      By now be out.
Yet, there's still a glow of 'other'
                    Like water running under ice;
Some echo of this quiet stasis still alive.
The gravel path is grayer and louder
                    Than other snows I've known.
I hear below the breathing epidermal dark,
          Not quite a pulse,
                    But a flow that's echoed in my veins.
I turn,
      And there, beyond the silhouetted guarding firs,
                The little space I've made:
(warmer than the icy moving wet I hear) *my home.*
My world is not an aquatint,
                    But gently growing densities of gray.
      There's yet some living Thales thing among the rocks;
Reverberating
            Reverent and
                Tender as a lover's touch,
Where corpuscles and throbbing seeds look forward to a
          STORM.
The colorless trees are winter-ribbed,
            and cage me like a lung
          That hungers for the surety of some huge
            Heart.

Thank God for nights,
          And the loneliness of nights.

                      Ellenville, December 9, 1983

Walking in Silence

    All love...all *life* is incomplete.
Two years...ten years...a hundred.
Every lifetime is stopped in or out of stride;
(it's not just unfinished, for *that* sounds like
we weren't able to ride it
                to an end.)
No. *Incomplete.* Because all *time*
Is incomplete...eternal or not.
We keep reaching into days and hours,
Unlocking clocks on the face of towers,
For any hidden second that would
                Stay.
Just as I wasn't given this gift of time
To change the world, but to change *me,*
So was I not given time merely to live it,
But to find and meet the One
Who calls me in it.

Surely the rain knows His name.
See how showers feed the flowers
And make a loveliness of mud.
The sun knows His name
And with a glance, draws from the green shoots
Only the colors that can dance.
Joy sits in the light and taps the tune
To tell the moon how lovely she makes the
night.
The moon knows His name,
                And it makes her lovely
bright.

They all know Him, though which of them will
say?

                                          February, 2007

To a Rose in October

It is that time.
The landscape is resigned; but there is fear.
Already your poorer friends
Have loosed and lost their petals,
Like hosts of weary butterflies, they dropped.
And see, the leaves, like herds
        They race and trace the roads;
Unfurrow fields, and cow at the fury of the skies.
Surely the wind is obsessed with dying.
Tomorrow will be sleep,
      Sere and sodden sleep……
            Till the brown bear yawns.
November will shroud what are left of leaves.
Though they may have died in a golden splendor,
                      They are dead.
But my heart has no November.
It is locked in the laughter of May.
It has walls and hills and valleys
                      Where no cold comes.
Where the wind is only remembered,
And never the sound of drums.
Its rage is the rage of cellos…..believe me:
      Though winters can be unkind,
Come rest in meadows past dreaming,
      The meadows of my mind.

                                              June, 2010

NATURE

The Sound of Summer

this sound of summer
bursting like the philharmonic
is illusion.
there is no drum-roll
in the perfumed peeling
of a rose.
it opens only.
still I have heard the children say
that a bubbling fire
will come with knocks as bright as blisters
on our doors this year.

late May, 1980

Impassive Stone

Some place in this impassive stone

I feel the ancient tremor;

even here the doe that turns in terror

finds her echo – as does the

startled fawn, the lonely child.

While yet the sun with pleasure warms,

the angle of her lines of light

makes cubes of fear along the rose's stem.

O in the clammy coldness of this stone

I find that we are one;

and the autumn glove of winter

is not enough to hide

the coming chill of death.

The Barn Loomed

                The barn loomed octagonal and black,
geometrically hard
        in the softness of the night.
By contrast
        the leaning silhouette of elm
seemed sure
        though bent now, by forgotten winds
                and other lights.
It seemed some studied carelessness,
        some lounging lift of logs and twigs,
            indifferent to the moon-tapped flow
                of streams.
Why am I here?
How am I here?
        in this place, oblivious to the heart's
                      time.
I know time and the passing robbery of days.
Though this mist erases clocks
        and the inexorability of their hands,
that sound of water in its endless flow
        is straddled for a space by
                God's simple sonic joke:
                the croaking frog.

        Perhaps its croaking is truer
                and tells more
than my heart can bear to know.
        He doesn't **see** the endless flow,
        but he **says** its passing.

                      August, 1978

Cape Cod

I was in light,
not water, bathed
here on this bay-binding slip
of crystalled earth;
here among the sea straw
blown ash and brown
by a silent hammering song
across my drying heart and hand,
I saw a lisping line of spray
and silver light
defeat the dumb and ox-like land.

Autumn

a crackling flame of flowers
in these fierce but furling hours
sparks the bearing wind
and spills vermilion fire
on a forest of flowing ambers.
what wonder grows
in the green wood, the back wood
where rack on the wrist could
from nature scream her dying
in your eyes.

all things marred
in the arson bright blight
of autumn.
where beauty's bellows
hard from enraptured hearts
blows the round breath of
awe.

O would death were always
bright and happy as the
ashes of this autumn.

1956

A Night Cry

The dark-lake cry of the loon

       Moans where silence and mists are found.

I wonder does he ever watch the moon?

       Does he know that if there is no man around,

For all his cries, he doesn't make a sound.

                                   May, 2006

A Web

confusing:

that a single strand of silk

from some grinning spider,

who stands astride his little world of night

and mocks centuries-strong sequoias

flushing them from focus

by simply being near.

he had seen the stars flicker in envy

when the close-kissed beam of lightning bugs

outshone the distant sparkle of some million light-years

journey to our eyes.

and so he spins his magic moment in

this fiery filament and gathers

all the light he needs to snare my lazy retinas in his web.

April 4, 2003

November Night at North Sea

    With stars and planets vying for the gift
Of any eyeball's turning,
                tempting the heart behind the eyes,
I stand electric in the surging dark.

   The wind is playing in the trembling place of trees;
shivering the dark to bright coitus in the night.
      the tremulous tracery of branches splayed against
                            the sky
and the sundered light of stars.

   Oh, how the wind now holds and wraps them
in its breath,
        stirring the sap in groins of rhythmic-tuning,
In the ecstasy of this night's bright and blistering
                        whispers;
Even while the inlet-lake is lapping against the stilly shore.

   Past the beating wings of all this leafy motion,
(which presses so against my breast,
        and brushes tenderly across my face)
are the remotest slivered lines of light we call the stars.

   I am at one with these things,
And know the harness of this most holy ground.
    I feel the gentle pressure of the bending grass.
and there those leaning lines
              of loft and lifting swirl of leaves
      dancing, writhing silhouettes
              of loving Nature in embrace.

NATURE

> I think they all were reaching for the stars,
> But held each other in their terror of the dark.
>
> If I were merely watching,
> I wonder why my heart was beating so...

November, 1974

The Catskills

    Through the lattice-bend of boughs
An amber moment burst like alabaster
                On the gloom,
To hint the space of home.
    Out there
  In the deep dell's dark,
A mist crept in from spools and pools
Of webbed, but not till now distilled, gray gossamer.
Fire-flies, like wading tugs of light,
Sparked their vaunting childish stars
Placelessly impotent in the silent power
                Of the night.
They spark too (these tiny tugs) the petty hope,
              The passing dream....
They poke the puniness of all us little things
Against the million-mile-dark and
                Make the dark give way.
Perhaps some black and purple leaves
              Take heart, and
  Remember for the blinking of the light,
Apollo,   or.....the naked Sun......
                Or JESUS,
And in Him, the Power and the Meaning
              Of a dream.

                              August, 1980

Is the Light Always Warm...

A baleful pail full of pleading tears,

Torn in turn from the mournful mountain

As this day died.

We cried always when late summer

Stole the laughter from our eyes.

No one knew but me and you

What all the laughter meant.

No one knew but me and you

How our spent hours were spent.

Who knows when summer goes

What happens to the light?

Who knows if the petalled rose

Is terrified of night...

It courted the sun its whole life long.

Could its perfumed song have been so wrong?

Clutching at rays it held so dear,

When only the warmth was ever near?

March, 2009

The Gulls

It inches, this untiring, lunar-tilting sea,
looping its lace,
from the white filigree lasso loom of waves,
parting the garrulous gulls.

They tip-toe in their tiny ostrich-mime,
dreaming big feet to make their marks
along the indifferent strand.
one spots something, unluckily foolish,
along the lisping lips of foam;
he darts and dips his beak, breaking in a trice
the malted-bubbles, to snatch the prize,
then strut with his strand-strut-head held high,
to say in beaming feather-walk: "Look at me."

1998

New England

carrying stones to crooked walls
is what the old settlers did.
O not in the mid-west: there the
stumps undid them, or they the stumps.

but here in the east where the
rocks protruded like frost
(not the ice-frost but the poet).
unlocking fields for seed
broke the backs of horses and of men,
and cost the country neatness
and straight lines.
but the land itself would not be
mocked,
or sit on stools for lion-taming farmers.
it would feed us...but in *its* way.
that spirit in the soil
seeped into its citizens
and made the Yankee.

February, 1990

The First Fall

the snow began disguised as mist,
stealth among the trees.
    the air was still as canvas
    before the painter sees.

once supple webs of greenery
grew brittle in the chill:
    their petalled sounds of color
    octobered to this mill.

the unflowering mill-stone, winter
was grinding in the mist.
    those tender scents of wonder
    which in wonder I had kissed.

the woods, once warmed with perfumed words,
turned silent without fright;
    for it knew in prisms and in prayers
    the mystery of white.

                            Ellenville, December, 1983

Fearful Notes

as white imprisomed all color,
and snow old memories of spring,
bells steeple the silence with hope.

I had heard you were afraid,
so my heart in haste raced
through the dance of dark
that was this waiting.

race, O reaching grace, across
this space of talent.
untense his fingers,
gentle them to his heart's height;
melt his fear to music
and make mild mock of his soundless locks.

uncertain still,
ring the strings and spark
these wicks of sound
to light.
unsilent time, past tone to telling
and to tears.

Nature's Gift

We have walked with wildness
                        In frowning forests
Where hidden waters sang, so soft
                        Among the lark-loud leaves.
At times they all would stop.
                        Then we could hear the bees;
Strange in a forest to hear the bees.
                        (Where were the petals and the pollen?)

Slyly the wind began to bugle,
                        Its cadent oboes called below the leaves.
Where bluebirds belled alarms to the startled wren,
                        But the purring bees purred on. And then....
                        Beyond the woods,

Flowers, like a field of lovely metronomes,
                        Waved their laughing colors in a rhyme,
And there in smiling sunlit hoods
                        Watched their blossoms burst to time.

Bracken along lethargic banks
                        By filigreed and friendly fern,
Turned in coolness from the sun,
                        And smiled to watch the daisies turn.
I felt some envy in my eyes
                        To see the wealth of such a place.
I bowed my head to nature's gift,
                        For there was a smile on her sweet face.

NATURE

Crossing on the Ferry

Between the razor-sleek slicing of the dark,

But froth-edged, with the broiling foam,

White-angry from the uncaring blades,

This moiling magic out from the ferry's stern

Leaping without hands to spit its fire-bubbled foam

Against the hull's indifferent silhouette –

Are the relentless turbines breaking the silence

Of the bay to bring us home.

August, 2005

A Shadow Speaks

I will always walk quite near you in the light,

Though some darksome god forbids,

And makes me disappear at night.

Walk in the sun, and I will follow you,

Not always at your back, but behind trees

And under rocks where I get my strength

To bend the backs of flowers,

And turn their faces towards the light.

The sun gets all the smiles and forces me to hide.

But I am to *turning,* what the moon is to tide.

March, 2009

Why We Like Flowers

    Death has a stench,
While life is in love with flowers.
Flowers at a wake may belong, but quickly cloy.
Their perfume knows the petals have been cut,
And all the rest is *seeming*.

    Flowers long for the light.
They wait upon the very edge of day;
And in the dawn embrace the dew to life.
They take and turn those diamond drops,
That jewelry of night
To warmer fragrance and to brighter ray.

    To thank their sister Sun,
They free her prismed bounty
Unlocking bolts of daffodils;
Then roads of rampant red,
Are hemmed in and held by the gentle lilacs
Pale and so sweet purple hue.
Rose and rhododendron,
(Though envious of a lily quietly lapping up the light,)
Nod in fresh obeisance to the day.
Others may shed lonely tears,
But flowers only laugh to be alive.

                                                              June, 2006

DEVOTION

The Sensuous Rose

He stands in the wild synagogue of the sensuous rose
Breathing apocalyptic fire!
Charged with a whip of seven cords
He drove out the leeching locust hordes
When zeal made meal of His desire,
Proclaiming the wild worship of the Three!

While far down in the dark Gethsemane
Of my alien eyes a memory weeps like a tired
Pilgrim,
As he sightless picks his way, immired
In the stagnant pools, thirsting for his home.
But for the fleshy blindness of our carnal eyes,
Our worlds would split when any rose explodes.

Blind me! Bind me! O Christ wind me
In the white stillness of Your trembling intensity.

St. Peter

>When Peter sat among his friends,
and soft-wicked candles with their flower flames,
gentled all their faces,
>>in a lens
>>>like Caravaggio's light;
caught clearer then, than Monet's or Van Gogh's photon-miracle
>>>>of unimprisoned sight.
>>He *crowed* his lasting love to Christ:
that *he* would never fail his friend or
>trade away his loyalty, by a fire,
>>>(whose warmth he'd take
as payment for his fear.)
>>But then the night would call him,
and three times he stepped away from knowing Christ.
>>And then....alone, in the dark of loss
his eyes remembered waves,
>>and the Light whose love had called him from the boat.
and now the wet was *in* his eyes,
and blurred his vision of the falling Christ.
>He felt the cold night's clutch;
>>and the cry from weeping friendship in his heart.
But now again
>those eyes were magnets whose mercy pierced
the black of elbows and whips and spit
to find his face and wash it with
>>>both their tears.
>>A different fire now burned in him,
and scorched the traitor from his eyes,
>>>the coward from his lips.

>>Again Christ's eyes
had fished him from the dark
>>>to let his tears soak through the loneliness of turning,
and find the stalk that was his name.

>>>>>>June, 2002

8:30 Alchemy

you lock your faith with laser looks,
not fierce like flaming eyes,
but gentled beams,
longing for a life *beyond* my words.
but you touch and spark that listening place
behind *my* eyes;
and in my chest.
Yet all the while
somewhere past the purple pain of grapes,
He leans unleavened in my hands.
and rolls your lovely lights into a ball
which only His heart's mitt can hold.

I used to see Him in a doorway
or along a curb,
a tin cup in His wounded hands;
waiting in the dampness for our love.
He thought the nails were cold,
until He held that cup.

But here in this small room,
your coin of love buys treasure
only He can change to gold.

April 2, 2003

To My Own Angel

```
         You never left me where I would have
               to lean     alone
                         andwailagainstawall;
      Nor took me and then forsook     me
                              in mists of my own making;
      To find my hell in my own dark dell,
                              Apart,
      Where no green was, or clumps and stumps
                              unseen
      would fake my feet and leave me
                              where      Ifell.

         Yet I never felt your hand.
```

January, 2005

After Night...

Then loomed the louring of that night,

The night when no dawn comes,

When all clocks stop, and untuned time,

Like hearts, will have no further beat...none.

When weeping dusk will know

That all her darling days are done.

Yet day, a *different* day, *will* come,

An undawned day all filled with May,

Not budding May, but full and flowering:

God's own day, (erasing all that's

Left of darkness and of night.)

A day of His, and His own Dear Son's Light.

                                                       March, 2009

Renewal

Wet as willow-white
In the tear light of morning,
In the sweat of night's labor to lift
The dark hand from the dead land,
We wait and are alone.

When wax in the shrill wind
Stops the sap to stone,
Fear sees the signs and whistles.
Again we wait. Again we are alone.

The old crier taps the windows of the forests
And tells them to shut down.
A mist sits hard upon the wicks of flowers
And worms have curled around the hours.
Yet we wait. Yet we are alone.

But in the ancient kneeling-house of incense,
Lodged among the plaster-molded men,
In sooted, flickering shrines
A Crucifix dimly plies the wind
With the unseen vision of renewal.

Blind as the Rain

blind as the rain, death walks without eyes.

    cold as the rain that chills us within;

that wells in our souls when it slips from the skies,

    and pierces the mind like splinter-glass sin.

hard as the rain, death hurls at my heart

    mist-moulded-missles that have flown through the years.

stark as the rain, death speaks out his part

    and laughs through the mask of time's saltless tears.

but so like the rain that scatters the mist

    (for after its fall there is sweet-blending blue)

death shatters the bars about eyes he has kissed,

    and at last I can hold   Christ in my view.

What We Dream

Our prayers impregnate the possible,

Turning our dreams to embryos;

And they, when fleshed in the womb of words,

Find their birth in what we say.

      But all along, unknown to us,

We are doomed to become our words.

      Sometimes we bleed in their saying,

Breeding something still-born and tragically inert;

      At others,

We hear the rush of wings,

            Recognize the dove,

See the branch he holds in his beak,

And know some land is now green and
                          waiting.
The silent storms may be over and gone.

      But *are* we what we dreamed?

                                  August, 2006

When Morning Comes

Before the dawn draws back the night's

Soft sable and so does-in Orion

And the bear he hunts,

A housecleaning morn sweeps up

The spill of Pleiades but slyly hides them, like some silver dust,

Under the corner of the day.

The morn was always false

And stayed too short a time

To make a job of it. Though every flower in every field

Turns to keep its eye on the deceitful sun,

Her dying magic merely mesmerizes them to sleep.

They simply never know.

Not so with us who know too well

The meaning of setting suns.

Still, like the hopeful one-eyed daisy,

We know our night will end.

And even in the dark we'll dream

A dream much richer than our day.

Is He

Brighter than bird-song

Much clearer than pain,

As lonely as wrong,

Or grass waiting for rain.

What was I hearing?

Why did I cry?

That longing so searing.

Still I don't try.

Where is His coming?

Is it easy to see?

Is it He off in the gloaming,

Or is He in me?

December, 2009

The Name

Is there one name that sums up all your life?

One name that calls up all your *love?*

That penetrates your darkness when alone?

The one that's on your lips when pain pushes

    All your other words away.

Does it lie beside you when nurses and rumors

    Crowd your room,

And open all your windows to the day.

In what treasured place do you hold it dear?

Is it your gentle breath that keeps it near?

    Say it.

April, 2005

Good Morning

"Good Morning," I said to God.

And waited quietly to see

If He in turn would spare the rod,

And gently turn His face to me.

I knew His eyes could always see

The leaves in autumn hit the ground.

God fends the forest and mends the tree,

But would He turn to my poor sound.

The earth itself has sliding faults.

They wait, then tremble, to setting mountains free.

God tends the heavens and all its vaults.

Isn't it absurd that He thinks of me?

February 29, 2008

HOLY WEEK

Kind King, O Jesus joy, and fire of friends;
Palm-pressed, though frond-freed but bound
By the beats, and bursting sounds of cries around
Your haloed hope that sends and rends with arms at ends.

To reach beyond the beach and held-in sea.
Who knew that black and bloody day would make a May
So soon replete with flowered saints? There were none could say,
Until a tall-tuned heart would toil with words that see.

Where withered wheat and shells like bells will ring
And bring the Father's men, hard fishing then, to weep.
There was no one in care or ken who ever thought of sheep,
Except the Lamb whose heart that day was opened wide to sing.

"O giving God, replace the rod which once had brought such pain;
Call out our loves, turn hawks to doves and make us whole again."

July, 2004

Last Night

Last night it was while veiled in censer smoke,
And saintly picture hung on me like honey,
I lifted head from hands and chanced to look
At him whose eye with love had seen me holy.

If holiness there were it lay within his eye,
For mind of me beneath this outward calm
Was loud with cheering.....I exalting me
Played hero to the crowd that filled my dreams.

O I am actor, spieling lines that have
The look of life, but empty is their ring.
Lord, poison and make bitter every spring
Of self that rises in the desert of my love.
Then rain in my Christ Your water's wealth
And drown my dryness in Your saving Death.

September, 1947

I wrote this the morning after my first night at the Seminary. It was just after Benediction and it became a door to the rest of my life. I always felt that it had the economy that truth demands.

The Annunciation:

No one heard the pressing-God against our sky.
Nor saw the feathered light leak through.
But a little girl turned from her work
to feel her sentence in a weight of words.
First fright, then tears….a smile…and then:
a sudden flush of fullness in her cells.
God-wrapped and wombed, her hand
pressed tenderly against her place of life.
The *'Yes'* man had hoped for, since the Garden, had been said.
Yet townsmen out of doors saw nothing new.
The ox continued his circle 'round the crushing stone,
Buyers bought, and sellers sold. But no one knew.

    Then a shepherd, in confusion,
    Watched a *shudder* moving through his flock.

Transfiguration

God, who is love, and lovers always want to speak to their beloved, spoke to *us* His Word, and His Word was Jesus. Now, in Jesus, the pure Spirit of God could *feel, feel what human beings feel. And more importantly, He could show in human ways His love for us.* Lovers always want to be understood. I said God is love. Inaccurate. God is not a **noun;** He is a **verb**. He is always lovING. His love is always ACTIVE. It is always GOING ON. And so His Love, Jesus, took on our flesh, and walked our ways, through towns and villages, through streets and alleys, climbed our mountains, and told us to watch: *"His feet are coming to us on the waters.."*

And in today's readings, once, He pulled back the Divine veil, and showed us, for a moment, our humanity Transfigured in the glorified body of Jesus. *Our* Jesus, one of *us*. His Body glowed with such brilliance that even His clothing became dazzlingly white. His grace never shone more beautifully, except hanging on the Cross where He paid for OUR beauty, for OUR Transfiguration. For this Transfiguration was also a ***promise.*** God was showing us in Jesus, where we were going. Jesus had said, *"I go to the Father, but I will come back, and I shall take you, US, where I am."*

That night, Jesus had with Him, there on Tabor, the friends of His Heart, Peter and James and John. He knew that they, these three, would be with Him during His agony in the garden at Gethsemane. This moment of joy was to deepen their faith so they could bear and share the agony. But their hearts were not yet up to it. They missed most of that Agony. They slept, and left Him alone.

Like them, Jesus won't condemn us for *our* sleeping, but, like them, we will also have left Him alone.

2009

Rosary After Mass

Lord, I hear,

(While talking to You,)

That gentle telling, that tolling,

The life-drone spell and spill of words

From their heart's cup, poured in pounds of sounds

To Your Mother's ears.

She hears. She Listens

To the hand held, heart-bound bell of beads;

The bouquet song of roses spoke in pleas

And plied from lips which lay their longing

In her palms, Christ-calmed and kissed.

Almost silent,

A faint scent of petalled prayer.

In unnamed morning moments this rite collects

Their cries and rightful-rough they follow Bread to Christ.

He'd have it so.

March, 2010

The Gift

How shall I say? What can I do?

What in all this world of gifts You gave, do I give You?

Where, when I walk the ways of beauty, is the place?

Where, an altar among the *all* of endless grace, find I Your Face,

To pour my paltry thanks and limping praise

To One who marks and loves my clay-worn ways?

It is the clay, from Adam and the earth.

In Your potter's hands that gives to me my happy birth.

But now,

The Garden gone, with part my fault,

Comes here across the sky's bright vault the endless tears

With my sad salt.

Twice it is, from earth's dry sand,

Once at birth and once again, I feel that Easter-touch of Your Warm hand.

I thank You Lord, in Your love's own way

You made us Yours from earth's dark clay.

Was it the clay that made you love us,

More then all the loves above us?

"Amen. Amen," I say.

September, 2008

THE MAGI: A JOURNEY

   It wasn't as though the sky was
overfilled with stars on that sudden cold
and moonless night, but something,
in the heavens must have moved,
been different..
               some piece of Promise shaped to light
fell hard as rocks on six uplifted eyes.
The boundaries of hope's containment broke
to free an avalanche of ancient prophecy.
               With hearts
pounding to the quasar quest,
the Magi sold their goods at home,
set businesses to fit the new time's order,
some family and friends heard unbelieved goodbyes
and a caravan of camels bore the unfelt
burden of prophecy.
Their leathern girdles on the swaying humps complained;
the jagged rocks beneath the padded hooves
seemed at first indifferent –
no distinction in the weight of simple goods
or
   Life-bearing dreams was yet apparent;
"For human hope is pottery or lead," they thought,
"It cracks in pilgrimage
            or breaks the bearers backs."
Still they set themselves to undertake the task.

               How hard
the journey must have been.
Most of the mouths that went cursed the
distance and the
           loneliness,
and hungered for what they thought was home.
For though our feet seem so for searching,

the heart wants home, wants roots,
wants earth....wants other hearts;
and only at last unpeels that one deep root
that makes all our searching steps but
an unknown painful coming home.

            For most,
they say it was a dark journey
    merely filled with work;
but for the drawn and driven Three
IT WAS THEIR WORK merely filled with journeying.

Oh yes, the Magi shared the dark,
but for them it had a crack.....a line of light
            broke through,
 And in some silver distant way
said, "Come!" said, "Yes!" said, "Home!"
said, "Hope!" said, Heart!"
          But still
how warm I wonder, is a tent
even filled with gold, or frankincense, or myrrh?
Only their hope of *giving* could have made
it warm enough.
   Though tents can be coldest,
journeys and caravans must also have their chill.
So then the Magi's sight,
        their eyes hope
spread out its warmth to other eyes
that slept alone in tents that knew no gifts.
And
  so the
     journey
        must have gone:

each man struggling in his heart for worth,
for value in this trek, for signs
and shapes to say that Hope was walking there,
or Truth, or that somehow they had strapped
some MEANING with all the weight they thrust
upon the groaning camels....to say
that ultimately hope was truer
        than their guts.

How many days or months
or was it years, that little crack of light
would flicker, and blaze, and fade,
and even turn their searching eyes to tears.
How many times their eyes and hearts
and arms held desperately each other
in love and loneliness,
      and the work of bearing Time.
Until
 at last
   a Stillness came.
At length they saw the Light hold fast,
and would not any farther go.
  Just
   THERE
      beyond the rim of sight
plain matter held a glow.
   There was no palace but the place was
        "other-warm."
They had not quested kings, nor found they
       courts of power.

A life of preparation –
       then this journey to a stall.
The smell of earth was there already and of dung,
shepherds and the smell of sheep.....
oxen like stones that had found the key
to some slight sightful unreflecting motion.

DEVOTION

    Their journey ended they stood in silence
            and they stared.

    For there a little girl leaned gently over Life,
like tears of wonder about to fall.

All that long journey's Light
          became but a moment in those tears,
          or welled within the eye,
          or curled along her tender lips
until
    a sudden once,
               without surprise,
they dropped like things long-loved and held at last.
They fell quite simply upon the shining
                Face of Light.
Was this the thing that once they saw in the
                breaking of the night?
They stood in silence still and stared,
and then they knelt.
    Then in some deep and human place:
          they wondered and they wept
at all the tears and all the work
that the telling of this night's tale would take.
      They had shared the moment and the glory,
now bear again the journey and the work to tell it's story.

                                          1956

Good Friday

Righteousness had killed Him,
                           and feigned misunderstanding.
               And always fear.
Such common and ordinary human acts to
                                 bring about a death.
But so it was and now the stone was set.

Behind the stone was the dark and stillness,
We saw and felt them as the stone was rolled in place
To seal the dark and the stillness.

For all the centuries this was the act
                that signed and sealed the end.
Tears and leaning on each other,
And all the other quiet acts of grief,
Could not undo the thing that had just been done.

Time had just been stolen from the stone.
Memory now, was all.

Yet unseen in this terrible dark,
                Hands were folding the face cloth
We knew was on His Face...
                And lifting up a sheet....

April, 2011

More than a Dream

I went once like an island people thought
    Was born in the sea.
Erupted they thought, from some horrendous depth;
    Now sitting there in this incense-bearing ocean,
    Like a baby Buddha.
But I wasn't.
    I only dropped a few inches,
    Past a stethoscope
        Into friendly hands
That then struck me. I yowled across the wet
        Like a piece of broken wind.
        Fragile as fright.

    Who knew that I would one day *call* God,
(actually *whisper*)
    Till He dropped from some heaven,
        Surely a light-year at least away.

Then I would break Him, (only because He asked me to!)

    Everybody kept watching,
        Looking at what a light-year had brought.
    But it wasn't the light-year that brought Him.

It was the *calling* and the *watching* and the *breaking*.
    Faith had broken the silence of centuries
    And forests fell away before that whisper.

The **watchers** didn't know how important
    The *watching* and the *breaking* was.
    But Jesus knew,
        He had heard their eyes *calling* in the *whisper*.

He knew that He must come *to be broken*,
    That the *breaking* was the **key**.

That it could unlock our dark and fearsome forests
        And turn again
To the gentle shade of the Garden we forgot.

Only humans and the Spirit can whisper so,
    And *here*, whispering is enough.

September, 2011

SEARCH

The Wrong Side of the Sky

you are after all

madam

on the wrong side

of the sky

to dig your garden

for such roots.

do you really expect to find

the feet of a tree

whose leaves are

stars?

O what great hearth

in you

sends clouds to make us sick

with longing?

really!

Songs I've Heard

The sound *beneath* the sound is what I long to hear;
Unwhispered songs with notes unsung, unheard by any ear,
Still is its breath beyond all death,
In an unseen silence I ever touch with fear.

The words we speak in voices loud, die swiftly in the air.
The din of action, though angel graced, can never now compare
With that sweet sound, in tears or laughter found,
    By poets born to care.

I must gather all my heart has heard, and in the skies
See blest my songs, where nothing dies.
And high among the highest birds,
In tears perhaps, I've found the words
    To sing the sound that cries.

July, 2005

A Soul Speaks

        Long before the stars, great capless jars
of shatter-night were set upon their black and arching shelves;
before the gaseous fire-girdled thing of light
                              had filled the vaults
        of then, and now, and time to be;
even then before the many moods of twisting seas
had kissed and killed the rock-strength sureness of shapeless shores,
You knew me.
        You held me in the ageless arms of Your thoughts.
You spoke and Your words were never-ending.
(For yet unborn, a toothless Time lay kicking
within the womb of everness.)
                You spoke and
in the very voicing of Your words Eternity breathed
a breathlessness to the inmost of my ear.

        O there was locking then of eyes,
                and touching then of ears,
and lips were mute,
                and all the space between.
For hearts sped out beyond the place of fears,
and drew their flaming redness
                      where love had gathered to a greatness
and would spill if touched by lips
                or hearts,
or even pointed spears.

        You knew me then and loved me,
and whispered of a way that I might follow.
A way where roses slept with thistles and where
the up and down of wimpled lips would even to the straightness
                            of a line.

SEARCH

>What then has happened to this way,
> the road and light that winds along the fence
> >where distance deals out days?
>
>>Has unwombed Time so quickly grown that now
> with hammer-smashing years He cracks the locking of
> our eyes and tears apart the touching of our ears?
>>Has Time, with soot of centuries, so blackened the
> stain-glass of my eyes that now they hang great hooded holes?
> While deep within I madly scratch for light
>>>and blot instead
> the grayness of my brain.
>
>>O Father, and Master, and Maker of me, Time Your tool
> has stolen the strength of Your child. Has islanded me.
> And there is only distance to wash through the sands
> of my soul....only distance destroyer of love.
>
>>My Father, O Lover of me, I am so alone.
>
> Eternity is clothed in when's and now's, and on my lips
> there is the taste of naught but space and time,
>>and distance bounds the journey of my soul.

>>>>December, 1947

Reflection

it was a moment by a mirror,

a fleeting one, for a passing figure.

I think the eyes were black,

blacker than the hair.

that's all I ever knew,

except the lips.

they never moved.

yet

I can never forget all the things they said.

January, 2005

The Alchemists:

Scoffed, cartooned, and caricatured,
They stood beside the phials and tiny etnas;
In boney fingers they clutched their maps of old,
And bent in darkness over their beakered dreams of gold.
With hidden hopes much brighter than the failing flame,
They toiled to take base metal, and in secret, change its name.
We mock them for that foolish dream,
Yet every day with fonder hopes and eyes that beam,
Standing in place where once they stood,
We take base deeds and try to make them good.
It is a work so often marked with pain,
For only God *starts out* and *keeps* the good;
We, having lost it, must search it out again.

August, 2008

When Quiet comes

With your tiny single-fingered hands impale the Time
And let the stroke be not in seconds but in years.
My feet are in the hour-glass, in so uncertain sand,
No longer lithe on shores, those margents of the world.

Feet like Aladdin's, but 'still-lamped' and mired in the shift,
Where grayer than grist, these specks give way
To gravity's unfeeling pull.
See how the grains, impervious to tears
Or other cries,
Follow their kind in an endless disappearing march.
Down they drag the deeds and breath of men
Much farther than just the waiting glass below.

I remember when I, with wild child's fierce fire,
Enticed by that world's shores, made my marks
Which made me laugh and giggle in the sun.
The gulls paid little heed, dropping their shells,
Dull bells, among the rocks, where steady but inattentive starfish
Stalked, in silent search for family
Or for food.

It was wide, the world I pressed, and longer than the eye.
The sky I saw, was nowhere to be touched;
And reeds, drab oboes, hummed unlarklike in the wind.
But I was *there* with steps that teased the waves;
And mocked the sibilant dark
In the sea's o'er stretching voice.

But here in the straightened confines of an hour-glass,
Caught now in these endless eddying grains,
There is an unheard rhythm that I hear,
There is a silver *quiet* becoming *now* more dear.

Darkness

Silence sits in the dark

Waiting for my eyes.

Darkness knows that every spark

Promises light. But sometimes lies.

When all the dark is gone,

Where does Silence go?

The din of day turned sunlight on,

Now mocks my whispers so.

November, 2007

Emptiness and song

So much pain and emptiness

    Have shaped words more beautiful than hills.

The tears in them enrich us more,

    Than does the dew on daffodils.

How can emptiness make

    Songs that are so rich?

I sit alone in this dim light

    Plying the secret switch,

And longing for a breathing next to mine

    With sounds sweeter than birds.

If this cannot be, then leave me so,

    But let me sing my grief with words.

              September, 2007

Aching

Once, I ached each morning, like a millstone for grist.

I rose like a raindrop out of the mist.

I longed like a mouth or an ear-drum for sound.

I felt in the night, the cool silence pound,

But heard through the dark a whisper-

There were wings around.

Does the rose hear some thunderous rolling of the sun?

Yes, why does it turn to follow, yet never run?

Why does it follow, is there a call?

Does *it* hear something that speaks to us all?

Could the One who made the seeds

And favored the earth He plants them in

Favor the mute and foster their needs,

More than the ones who think Him kin?

Silence

Darkness is the silence of the eye,

As silence is the darkness of the ear;

Yet both find joy when the tongue sings silence

Into words that stir and light the dark.

O Father of the Word, who spoke aloud Your Son

That we might have joy, pressed down in everyone,

Grant me the ear to hear Your steps in snow;

And let me see in silence the dark that has Your glow.

July 3, 2009

"80"

If I had known their richness and their wonder,

When Time was dealing out my callow days;

When poetry and love, unthreatened in their thunder,

Held *unseen* the promise of their ways.

If I had seen the worlds inside the casual words,

And heard that fiercest music, when they were said,

Would I have opened up what my heart girds,

And let the rush of love come in instead?

If so, would now, my heart, with memory, be sad.

That in each of my budding years, (a score)

There came to me the thousand gifts I had;

Now know that *all that was*, I shall have no more.

Or was it wiser, in poverty, not ever to have known

The worlds of love and wonder that in the years have flown?

March, 2009

How Cider Lasts

Wounded hearts had waited while the fat of heart were sated,

Where the questioners in queues only waited for some news.

But the answers never came.

We prayed there all the same.

Lonely men forced on by need

Hear the warnings but pay so little heed.

Mountains look like valleys when you see them from above.

Dangers wear a welcome when you're looking out from love.

Most of the mad ones are rarely locked away.

It's the innocent unlucky and their children who must pay.

When Adam added cider in that garden there about,

He heard a voice of thunder and by thunder he was "out."

Actually I should say:

Not *he,* but **they.**

For *they* had grown complacent (as anyone could see).

The world they might have saved for us, was lost by a little *'me'*.

Obeying seems so slight a price for a Garden grown that sweet.

But think before you blame them, since you and I repeat

The very things that drove them out,

And put us on *this* street.

April, 2008

Light Without Shadow

    I stood there, my shoulder against the years.
When I looked up
    I thought the stars were tears.
Where were the ways, I wondered,
    To work my steps through fears?
There was dark at the top of the stairway.
    Black was under my feet.
My heart kept urging, *"Onward."*
    My mind kept saying, *"Retreat."*
Light can't *only* be inward,
    I see it in eyes, as they turn.
I feel it in hearts reaching outward,
    They touch, and they hold, and they burn.

"Fear not." A voice with white wings.
    "Let not your heart be troubled,"
Came again from the lyric link of wings.
    My *"Yes"* that had lain so mute
Comes now from a heart that sings.

                        June, 2006

To My God of Silence

I was standing in those dim eighty years

With eyes that never heard Your steps.

But tonight the quince has offered its own incense

To the big-as-birth rhododendrons;

And see the rose, smug as ever,

With elegance like tea-time, waits its turn to open,

t h a t a l l t h e w o r l d m i g h t s e e.

    Even the Sun, in particular wonder,

Held this petalled thing in the womb of its warm hands,

        until,

Primed for parturition, it burst in fragrance on the air.

    O Yes. You *were* there.

                              June, 2006

Morning...

       In the morning my eyes
So slowly say their *yes* to light.
My body longs for strength
      To tear away this blanket's warmth
                      Or womb.
And yet my heart sits firm on the edge of day.
      I know I'll shower
             And shave the residue of
                        Yesterday,
And a thousand other hours.
      For the night's soot, the invisible grime
        Clings to the skin of who and what I am...
          Darkness eventually always goes –
Though I have known some light
      To be too sharp and edged
            And even have a boulder-weight.
Some days the sun destroys the tender petal,
Bends the blossom and breaks its beauty's sheer
                     Sweet sinew.
      But there are no flowers
Nor any lingering luster to the earth without
                    The sun.
      Without the fearful risk of each day's dawning
There is no other warmth.
           Except perhaps for love.

                              February morning, 1973

Among the Palms

It was around mid-day. A few merchants who had just come back from Bethany were delighted with their sales and with a little tidbit of gossip about the Wonderworker they had all been talking about. Even some of the leaders here had begun, if not to follow, at least to show great interest in Him. But what was the gossip? One of the more successful merchants had a somewhat slyer look about him; and his voice certainly changed when he began – with a look over his shoulder – to share his tidbit from the trip. "Well," says he, "this Jesus was at Simon's house, *Why* He should have stayed at Simon's I haven't the foggiest idea. I guess Simon was having some friends over. It was a kind of party but a very quiet one.....some talk...a few laughs. Mostly people came to see Him. O He was *there,* and I think He paid for it. Just after supper – we were all relaxed – when in comes Mary. You all know Mary; I'd say some of you know her *better* than others. All right, so *I* knew her too. But bold as brass she comes up to Him. Right in front of everyone. You could hear a pin drop. She kind of slithered up to His feet. She knelt there for a moment, her long hair touching the floor. Then she started weeping all over His feet. She grabbed some of her hair to dry them. Imagine, her *hair.* Then some ointment. Beautiful smelling nard; must have cost a good bit, I tell you. Some people started to snicker, till one of His own complained it could have been, *should* have been sold. Money to the poor, and all that. The big guy, Peter, gave him a look that would shut anybody up. So did John. I always liked John. But just then I tell you it was getting out of hand, really tense, so I left. But you'll all hear more about it. I heard they're coming up to Jerusalem."

The words were barely out of his mouth when you could hear some people gathering by the west gate. Someone yelled, "He's coming." "The Nazarene's coming." The word spread quickly. The excitement burst through windows and doors. Alleys began to fill up. They just added to the crowds that had come up for Passover. But *here* the mood had turned happy.....happy laughter..... happy calling. It was going to be a great day. Some were yelling, "Remember what He did for Lazarus!" "They say he was truly dead.....the tomb actually stunk." Someone added, "He must be coming up for the feast."

There were some women on the road after them, just a little ways behind. *They* seemed confused, some were smiling, eyes all bright; but a few of them seemed pale and worried. I wondered, with all the excitement, *why?* I think one of them was His Mother. "O My God, *there's* the one who draped her hair on His feet. And the ointment. They said she was a bold thing. I guess they were right.....but *look* at her.

The crowd was getting nearer and much louder. There was a lot of shouting....."HOSANNAH"... it was mixed with "It's Him." "Go, tell Aaron." "Somebody better go to Caiphas and let him

SEARCH

know." To which another said, "You don't think he doesn't know *already?*" "You can bet he does." The Hosannas got more frequent, and now people were throwing cloaks in His way, all along the path in front of Him. They all were struggling to reach out and touch Him. I never saw the like of it. Even the damned donkey looked excited. Where'd He get it from? Then the palms started. People running past us, back and forth and breaking off, *tearing* fronds from the trees. They were in a mad, happy, excited rush. In fact, we were swept up by the crowd to the edge of the biggest woods in Jerusalem, except for Gethsemane. They kept pulling them off the trees and running back to the crowd with them, some just waving, others throwing them before Him. Children were even climbing the trees, tearing pieces off and throwing them down to their parents, or for that matter...to *anyone*. Everyone was shouting; some even were calling Him "King"....and *Messiah*. I actually heard someone in a rather loud whisper, "He'll get rid of the Romans for us! These damn soldiers. They've been here too long."

Then this fat guy, running for more palm, knocked me against a tree. I lost my balance and went down. Somebody tripped over me; I thought he broke my ribs....thank God somebody else tried to help me up. But while I was down I could hear, somewhere in back of us. Not all that far, an axe cutting into a tree.....*chomp....chomp*. It wasn't palm, sounded more like cedar. He wasn't alone either. There must have been almost a dozen. Suddenly I thought, "Good Lord, they were soldiers. Roman soldiers doing their own cutting......No, *they* were just overseeing it. Some slaves were doing the actual cutting.

An explosion of Hosannas burst through our concentration....We turned back to the crowd. God, they were so happy! But just then the soldiers began to curse at the slaves, "Put a move on! We haven't got all day." They sure were impatient, stomping on the fallen palm fronds or kicking them out of the way. From where we were, we could hear and see the last stroke on the tall cedar. It tottered a few seconds then *smash*! There wasn't a lot of dust, the night and the place were too damp. The smaller cedar was already down. It was about six feet; the other was twice that.

Now they began flogging the slaves in earnest to get the trimming done. One of them had an adz and seemed to be squaring off the sides of the smaller trunk. I said, "We're getting too close. They are going to spot us, and then there'll be hell to pay." We backed away, into some denser bushes. That brought us back nearer the shouting. The Hosannas! and the joy of the crowd seemed to drown out the adz and the axes...even the cursing of the soldiers. Funny, I couldn't get that wood out of my mind. As I walked home that night I wondered what they were doing. Why all that time on a couple of cedar trees. Two pieces of very heavy wood.....They weren't even the same size.

June, 2004

Won't You, My Dear

Won't you, my dear,
                Come over here.
Together we'll sit by the fire.

We'll laugh at the days,
                And our frivolous ways
With friends we came to admire.

Our youth was so strong,
                With nothing *too* wrong.
We tasted all wines with our laughter.
We turned to the skies
                With challenging eyes,
Nor cared for the woes to come after.

The cafes we're told
                Were icily cold.
Winds blew through to the marrow.
But coffee *out there*
                Held more than its share
Of the plans that we made for the morrow.

We thought of the dream
                We stirred with our cream
While we drank, in the warmth of the sunlight.
How could we see
                That dreams cannot be;
Unless they were blest with the One Light.

But the One that was shown
                Was the One we would own,

SEARCH

The One that shattered the dark.
We walked in His praise,
                The rest of our days.
As we soared to the song of the lark.

                                    August, 2005

Moistened Clay

Do not see only Jesus in my eyes,

Or only hear His voice when I turn to speak.

Hear the distant times when I waited, or loved, or wept,

When I longed for the dawn in nights I never slept;

Times I might have felt the Potter's hands,

And gloried in the knowledge I was

Clay.

And the tears, Oh there *were* tears, not every day,

But thankfully, enough to keep me in my errant clay

Quite moist,

And pliable in His warm hands.

Tears in that awe-filled dark where I slowly learned to trust.

They kept me from (I think) too soon becoming dust.

July, 2008

Innocence

Is the hand withheld, less guilty than the one that struck?

If our eyes behold the wounded and our hands do not,

Can we ever be innocent of the blood we've seen?

Can innocence ever be passive?

How often we do betray our eyes.

If the hand is closed, can the heart be open?

No. No more than a question can be the answer.

There are thieves on other roads than the one to Jericho.

We can lose our step on any street and fall in any lane.

Can one ever hear a cry and claim he didn't hear the pain?

Is convenience ever worth the lie?

September, 2007

Questions 101

How much of laughter is really crying?
How much of life is really dying?

Is every taken-for-granted breath
A quiet step to an unknown death?

Would knowing it change the way we talk?
If we saw it clear, where would we walk?

Does knowing help us to prepare,
Or does knowledge bring but deeper care?

Is the distant scene a goal we set,
Or the unclear challenge that must be met?

Every hour has its own door,
Stay safe behind, or seek for more.

In love's mystery are we most at home,
Searching with Jesus through earth's dark dome?

April, 2011

SPIRIT

Silence

Silence is the mind's air and spring; it is its pasture and its grazing; it is the balm that heals, the water that nourishes, the supporting soil; it is the peeling of the seed, the multifoliate tongue of nature and the deepest voice of man.

There is that intense silence, broken only by pain, of a mother massing herself through a fist-clenched stillness, to that moment which will spark forever, with a cry, the age-old touch which Michelangelo unfurled across our sky.

There is the silence of counting a new baby's fingers and tracing the shape of his nose, and feeling his fragile ribs; there is the uncertain silence, not unmixed with timidity and awe, when we see the tiny pulsing at that delicate spot on the skull.

There is the silence of the infant, reaching with his eyes, to the tips of his world, an untried arms-length away. The arm will lengthen, the world will grow and the silence will change. It will become more seeing, more understanding, more contemplative, deeper and more painful. His cry which broke the barren ages and shocked him into being will not be the last of pain, nor the last of joy, not even yet the last of beauty hard to bear.

There is the locked silence of the child when he is misunderstood and the equally mute one when he feels he <u>is</u> understood; the silence when he finds that he can read, and when he first discovers the veins in leaves, faces in the clouds and great stories in the shapes of rocks. There is that wide silence the first time he sees a great deed and the narrow one when first he looks upon the face of evil; then that bubbling silence when first his hand touches the hand of love and a Transcendental blisters through his blood - and he is mute.

There is the wrinkled silence of the old wife who sits beside the window listening for steps; the compounded silence of her years of listening which did not avail, so that now, even though she knows that he can never come, that unsuppered hour of six and the lonely one at nine and the sobbing midnight still conjure up the fear which carved this silence, beside which she sits and under which she bends.

There is the tired silence of the gutted and guttered old man with his bag of rags, his bedraggled and bearded stillness, and eyes no longer waiting - walking a length of street that he can never out-walk, or out-last, or live beyond.

There is the roaring silence of war and the children who have never come to be because their fathers were too tall, or straight or weak or honest or afraid or brave. There is the rolling turbid silence of the sea, spraying in the wind, against unfeeling cliffs, the cries of a thousand armadas, and the watery blood of the men who danced their rigging.

O there are other silences like the silence of the sky and hills purpled into stillness, the silence of the Church, and the silence of Holy Saturday when the Light had gone out and then the silence of coming to the tomb; but most of all there is the silence before a door, the silence that stands before the gate and knocks, that silence to which all things open and reveal themselves, the silence of wonder and awe, which is one with the fragility of the rose and the cupped wonder of children's eyes, one with compassion and with nature and with God.

Seeming Death

     I had not seen this death in me,
for it seems the dying never see the inner-end
themselves.
    It comes as stillness comes,
or twilight, or rather like those running roads
that slowly leave the sea and fold the rock-sprung
sound of surf in the steady hum
of rolling rubber motion and the tedium
of quite ordinary turns.
         But suddenly
it's there - a kind of death - at no particular spot,
not even an event; a condition rather, that others see
and try to warn us of. But we cannot hear
and will not see.
      Or perhaps the fear
of having to admit misreading monotony
for meaning, pattern for purpose; admitting that
our caution was convenience and fear or risk
had paralyzed our deepest love,
is too much to expect.
         And so we die.

But I know there are Easters and the rolling
            away
of stones; that another human breath quite close,
or pulse, or touch,
      may be the three-days voice
that calls me to the light and stands with me
along the shore again to feel the face of spray,
           and life
            and wet

SPIRIT

    and tears that in embrace will mix with mine
          and give me back
             myself.

                                1970

Death and Dreams

        Death and dreams,
    Dreams and death
    Death *in* dreams...
But are there dreams in death?

    Why is there that madness in the moth,
      That makes it dream the phoenix dream
And flutter without fault against the unfeeling flame?

Does all light, luring us through the dark,
      Only take our powdered flight,
      Our fragile beating vans of hope,
      And in a silent unpiercing scream...
      (Heard only in the spheres)
          turn them to ashes...unfossiled
          and ugly in the melting wax of time?

Are we the dreamers or the dreamt?
Is it God's failure or our fault
        That the names in dreams don't always fit the dreamers?

Or is there fault at all:
    Are there *only* dreams?

Is all our dying deathless, and the phoenix the only fact?
      After the flames –
    Does the moth, in fact, know more than hearts:
        That dreams are never wrong?

                                          June, 1979

A Certain Moment

All time is past…..except
        For the moment we are in,
  This *now*.
The words that I am speaking,
        Even as they are said,
    Are past…not gone…but past
The not-yet…the unseen….the unheard
        Coming of the future
  Is *where*,
      and *when*,
          and *why* we wonder.
We have only the hints from things
    That were.

With all the weight of Time's immensity,
        From the big bang
  Till now,
The *second* that we are *in*
        Seems so slight a gift, at best.
Yet in the lungs and for the breath
        It is, I swear, worth all
  The rest.

This lived moment is the only place,

        To feel for God, and find
  His Face.

                            February, 2007

Silent Cay

    Life is such a thing of hope.
                       yet
    Young men
        never see the hand, whose pen
    Presses them from farms, and wives,
                And mothers,
    To fall in some unpronounceable puddle of dark sound,
        And unfeeling sand, hot, and
        Reddened by their stolen days.

        In helmets that smugly undark the night,
    Their light was ripped from a sound that
                Only others heard.
    Their buddies missed their silent cry.

        We never heard their dying, *"Why?"*

                                              November, 2007

Hope

Night had nailed her darkness to the main mast

                                 of the moon.

       But in the torrent of a splashing sun

I saw it sink in awful waves of light.

       All was swallowed up by morning,

Save the sable cats of her, that creep

       In every haunt where rivers of the dayspring

Never reach.

       My dreams had dried with the drying drops

Of night.

       And there, in the stillness of the dawn,

While stumbling hours waited for their call,

       I bugled out my garrisons of Hope.....

                                         March, 1949

Meaning?

      Must I everywhere behold my 'roots'
and still not hold that root of things
which my uprooting mind, to hold itself,
      MUST hold.

      But are there roots at all, or only things?
What weight on innocence do I impose with meaning?
    Do I reveal, or merely wrap the mysterious thing I touch?
Is THAT its recognizing voice I hear
        when from the dark I sense a name?
Or is the dark an emptiness
        which echoes back my name?

     In the un-noted music of light
         kissing itself to dew on dawning buds,
            or yawning yellow petals,
the melodies I hear.....ARE there!
A Piper
        quilled or skilled that endless silence into
          sudden SOUND.

And all my life I'll seek Him.

                                March, 1986

Inklings

What does the black-eyed susan see?

Who makes the somber iris smile?

Is there an archer for the bow that bends the rain?

Who repairs the broken grass where deer have lain?

In the *'real'* there are corners, around which

Only the eyes of the soul can see.

Questions are always on the lids of honest eyes;

And comfort is not where the searching heart should be.

Could I catch him, the doer of these deeds,

Before the wind can hide him in the light?

I only hear him when he whistles through the reeds,

What is day to him can be our longest night.

Speak in my darkness, Lord, your silent voice.

Light in my silence, Lord, your least lightsome rays;

But smile as you pass by, a hint to my heart,

Then I'll know you at last, in all of your ways.

September, 2010

On the Port Jefferson Ferry:

      some years, even some loves,
      somehow
      have more scars, with less effect,
than these white wakes on water;
            where air, split and spumed from
      the wet green, leave but for a moment,
            the milky wounds of passing.

how unconcerned
      this up-minded churning movement;
      in and out of sight,
            in and out of myths,
                  in and out of lives and...life;
      less than the uncolored music of seaweed.
            its only constant:
                  dark passing
                        and motion
                rarely understood.

                                  July, 1994

Mirror

    I am not the face looking back at me.
O mirror, of short memory,
Are these the eyes that caught a bird in flight,
Or tracked a ball to make a hero of my hands?
Why did they cede their luster to uncaring night,
And bury that brightness in dim and listless sands?

Time took it all away, for just so many years.
Most things seem less important now. True?
Once, there was a heavy price for tears,
Now any cold or winter wind will do.

Lids that shadowed out the noonday sun,
Or closed, to hide blind fury's wrath,
Or give some passion a quieter place to run,
Now, are grown too weak to hold the hero's path.

    Lips that let the singing lines of poets live
And sang aloud of Jesus and His friends,
Seem to have learned some deeper notes to give,
So, indoors and alone, I make amends.

I have bottled tears and laughter in one glass.
And all the fancied dreams that flow from every book.
Smilingly, I give away all the little things that pass.
To catch in silent wonder, my searching Father's tender look.

                July, 2006

Brooks and Leaping

Are brooks ever really *too broad for leaping?*

For the unathletic, perhaps.

For the lethargic, or the nodding, always.

For the uninspired, what's *leaping?*

For the hopeful and the daring,

When the prospects of leaping are dim;

They never watch from the sidelines,

They simply learn how to swim.

March, 2009

Walking in the Snow

Today I walked a country filled with snow

And with her silence spoke.....the two of us alone.

How much akin we were, only earth and I will know,

Since love will save her sorrow for her own.

I had taken me apart for I was sad,

And sought the silence of the snow for my relief.

I wandered thus about, half-weeping like a lad

Who knows not the reason for some young grief.

"How tranquil and at peace you are," thought I

"Even now when winter weighs on you."

In that symphony of silence I heard her soft reply:

(beyond the steely prism of her white, a hue.)

"The ice today that makes my world a tomb,

Will melt on the morrow: sweet fruit in my womb."

February, 1951

Tears

Tears, like painful prisms,
Can touch to light and telling
The colors of our too-tender dark.

Tears, the echoing chambers
Wherein we hear the silence,
Those unspoken hopeless crackings
Of our world's despair.

Tears can bend the light
And so compress and gather wounds
Too wide for the mind to hold;
into that healing place
Beneath the low-lintels of our hearts.

Give us tears then –
Not of our anguish only –
But tears for *meaning*
And of hope:
Tears that have the smell of slums;
Colorless ungettoing tears
That water loneliness and show us brothers.
Give us tears to fall on the shriveled face of cancer
As we hold the dying hands.....
O give us Theresa tears, those moments in
Emptiness
Of holding and being held.
Tears that hear and carry home
The one wealth that makes us *us*.

Tombstones

Looking out the window

Of the train from Ronkonkoma:

We were passing Pinelawn Cemetery.

I saw in stone a few histories all lopped of days;

They were the ones, burnished and still shining,

Whose dates and words cried out against their time.

The grayer ones, weather-chipped and rough,

Where words were muffled in the smothering moss,

Still mumbled to the wind the letters someone carved,

In loss, so long ago.

Names, much truer than their breath,

Take very long to die.

July 5, 2004

english III

that first time round, how much of joy there was

in watching the young faces light,

electric in the high tension of discovery.

pointing to the knobs, or the door-sill lights

of other rooms, of hidden brighter rooms, I stood close by

and saw the growing light steal in, and even

sometimes burst on the beardless face of awe.

O this was not every moment, but there were many moments

as bright and clear as new medals struck, or the

first sweet song of understanding in another tongue.

I saw in the noise, and the running, and the dreams

of that unencumbered single level which was their

youthful playing ground, a slowing, then a pause,

then a turning, and finally that incredible moment of meeting

when the boy reaches into the world of light

and burns his blood with truth.

there could be no other thing, this side of Sacraments,

I told myself, so replete with power to recreate the man

whose voice and eye were instrument to this end.

June, 1960

When They Meet

The part that breathes in me,

That works in me,

Is different from the part that cries.

But there are moments when they meet,

These parts.

And then I hear my name.

And *know* myself.

And I weep in the pride of my own terror.

2004

After Gertrud von Le Fort:

To the Church:

    Mother, your ministers have made
    a smiling but smothering mask of you.
    They have made me so safe that I never knew
    the black and cosmic things
                     in my coffee or with my eggs.
    why, when I was small, did they tell me not to ask;
                 that *all* I needed *they* would tell.
    and when a question blurted out, you metamorphed yourself
                 to be the answer.
    you robbed me of my fear of being lonely; when all I felt,
                 or saw or heard of
    told me I was alone. You kept me from the precipice of dark
                 which makes a question true.
    You always left your litany of lamps beside my bed,
                 and never completely closed my door.
    questions formed from fear are really friends; *they*
                 are lanterns in the unadmitted dark.

    You only had to *tell* me I was safe; not rob me of the
                 terror which waits in every human
                 street......to wrestle me for my truth.

But Mother, I thank you for your hand.

                                                July, 1996

Dryness and Tears

Do we contain in this moment everything we are? If not, what happens to the unlived things, left over, from some particular hour? Am I *still in* them; do they belong to *me?* Or is time simply like fish-roe, expecting only a few of its own to live? Where do we keep the parts we keep?

What makes the hours which are *coming*, heading right *for us,* try to fit the works of our hands? Or do they? *Given the time,* would we erode like some dried canyon wall, polished smooth by a hundred million unremembered moments? I suppose *that's* the difference. *WE* erode from the *inside*, without winds or torrents; only a pair of listless lungs and white cells losing their wars to slowly stagnating pools of red.

Something stops the synapse-snapping sparks whose nano-second-glow, burns brilliant in our eyes. The sparks cannot find each other now, and in the ensuing dark, all familiar streets and posts are gone. We who *were*, now frantic, like the eyes of children lost and searching in a massive mall gone gray; we *stumble* less and less but *fall* ever so much more.

In the busy world outside, no one seems to notice. All the ears that held our words, all the eyes that reflected laughter from our own, have now gone dry. Is *dryness* the enemy? Is this the traitor silently invading our cells? Shuffling, uncertain steps replace the stride. The *outside* doesn't do that to us. The wind doesn't do that. The rain doesn't fall inside; it cannot get there. Some of us seem to have some unseen gutters around our shoulders and our heads, that catch another's tears hidden in the rain, and make all the masks and human motion sluice through drains and wash away.

Yet *inside*, little parts keep going home.

How does time get in? It must have been there from the start when it smiled through the eyes of my kindergarten friends. So we wanted it too, as a *friend.* In all our boyhood games it played with us. But it was always faster than we could run. We just slowly lagged behind. When we stopped to pick some flowers, or paused to hear the breakers on the shore, time, like the sun, seemed so bountiful. Light and love filled up the days we thought would never end. We had no sense, with ice cream running down our chins, the collie chasing after sticks, and the stoops, clearly made for stoop-ball and not for climbing at all; we had so little sense how much of all we saw would lose *their* race. Dry days would trample all those lovely leaves which screamed through unknown colors as they died. Time merely watched, then turned to beckon snow. October was always lovely sad.

As our tears explode so copiously in joy, so do they run a silent river in our grief.

Before tears curled along our lids, licking up the soot of lashes, they were the pure warm prisms that once held all the colors of our lives. They are sometimes crushed from our hearts by the meaning and the weight of words we hold too dear for saying. Indifferent time pours equal salt in those that shine the cheeks of bursting laughter; as well as those that weep in silent, lonely desperation. Are they not the top and bottom of our pilgrim lives.....of all the light and dark we know. If we think that we have never heard Christ weep, just hold a mirror to your eyes.

August, 2003

My Father

The years: when I heard the music, even recognized the music,

    but could not remember the words;

The months: when I stood on a stretch of beach, in a mourning fog,

    feeling the agony of spray, able to imagine some unremembered terror;

The days: when I waited on the lips of the sea, aching to hear

    the sea's deep voice in my veins;

The hour: when fear froze me at that corner which my dead father had

    already turned. Yet sometime later, in surprise I swung my eyes,

    but it was he looking through them. He was standing in my feet.

    My lungs breathed *his* breath.

For in the end: things do not begin or end; they

    rise and fall, swell only and subside. There is no death: loss is

    but the unknown door whose silence is another tongue.

Stillness and silence stare through the grave, but they are

    gracious in their gravity and wait (with a warmth I do not

    understand) to teach me the words.....to tell me the Word I never

    really knew. (Now the words betray my tongue for never having heard.)

I meet myself in silence, but it is my father....or...you.

    He tried to whisper the secret that was his name but the grass

    was louder.......thunder even rolled from the rose. We never heard.

        How could I know the hand he rarely held

            could never let him go.

Here Along the Rim

here along the rim

of this unreal world

a solitary surfer

lolls on the back of a dreamlike swell,

Vermeered to stillness

on the oil-slick ocean skin.

the surf is muted now,

its echoes moistening in the sand.

I watched his easy poise intensify

until a sudden but so slight energy

burst to motion.

he climbed to mount the leaning line of force

sweeping toward the beach,

but like a steed of too great power

it slipped quite insolently by

and left no lift of spray

at the point of its encounter.

ARTIST

To Vincent

That little bit of bloodied ear drowned out your palette

and made the light a clashing cymbal.

the things you saw were never there,

until your fingers found them hiding in the light,

where people without your pain never thought to look.

the sun could hardly make you squint, but how it burned.

Tahitian color was too thick and lush with sap

for your poor brush that wanted only light.

Who knew in Arles they lived in such a place?

orchard-lovely and loving light, those ballet buds

would dance like laughter on your eyes.

You always heard their tinted music,

and caught the notes in colors never seen;

but you never heard the laughter,

with crouching madness hiding in your tears.

Now our eyes see only the orchards and the stars.

but it was you who knew the night..

Pebbles and Teaching

It was my great pain
That being small I still knew
What greatness was,
        And how to say it,
                And how to give it life.

I took pebbles a little
        At a time
  From that mountain in the mind,
And I threw them
        One
      By
            One
Into him....
        Into his soul...
Until
    They dammed up every crack and stream
Of littleness,
        And the man in him
Became deeper and
            Deeper
Until
    It could be pent up no longer,
And B U R S T out.
  O God
It bore him past me like a torrent
        Past a weeping boy
Looking for some place else to throw my pebbles.

                                      June, 1972

A Word

that shape of sound,
lipped and tongue-curved
out of living breath,
is false with seeming-life,
and falls upon the ear
already dead.
time which was it's present
is fleeter than the sound.
before it is heard, the words
are past.
I listened in the sequent silence
at the dying of a word
and with a sadness deeper
than the sound, I heard my
death.
so small a space my life,
no longer than my breath.

After Peter's* Class....

nothing knows what fingers know,

except perhaps the clay.

to it and them touch is loving,

and all the space around - a womb.

life doesn't hide in the clay.

it only waits.

tenderness will wake it;

so let our hands be tender

and knock against its silence as lovers do.

arcs and angles hold the form

and in the form: the breath.

Only God gives simply,

lesser hands must give and take

until the breathing

finds a home.

I have heard: musician's ears are feathered to their hearts,

gyred, they say, tighter than a hawk.

well so is the heart of God to sculpting fingers bound.

*Peter Rubino, sculpting instructor at the National Academy of Fine Art.

Day-done and Dark

Day-done and dark,

        As the last spark of our 'setting' one

Makes amber now the embers of her fire,

Lord, where no night lingers;

        Where the words of Way, and Life

Find flowers, ready in red bowers, and petals

all strife-strewn, are here blown dry to die

            among the cawing rook-singers.

Ringing bales of scales, in pealing praise,

amaze at last, like laughing tears, the brook's all dappled rays.

You sit here, stay here, on rocks of gray array,

      Far from John or Jordan or the Voice You heard that day;

Remain here, where *we* still fish, do all our ordinary things,

But wish one day to meet You on the rocks, or

            there among the trees, which once You used

            to make us whole.

Le Jongleur de Notre Dame

    The little juggler had only baubles to toss in the air.
He did it with the sadness of someone very poor.
He didn't dare to lift his eyes; but if he didn't
He knew he would drop the balls and they would fall.
And then his gift would be gone.
    And so he dared.
He lifted his tear-filled and frightened eyes
    To track the balls.
And suddenly, *there,* at first just for a second,
Beyond the highest ball, he saw her smile.
And then he loved the baubles and
    Knew that he was rich.
        His tears were different now.

    So should I love the words I search and toss
Up here, over there, or down
              Some tearful alley
To find the hidden notes that make them sing.
It is so slight a song.
    But it's what I do.
I haven't *seen* the smile.
        I just pray it's there.
Still, when I feel a note,
    That day is fair.

                      September, 2010

The Park Bench

I remember the blossoms.
I remember the snow,
And that time when the seasons
Seemed gentle and slow.
The bark was much brighter,
The trunk was quite small.
Though I stayed the same,
That sapling grew tall.

Couples nestled on my back,
Under starlight and sun.
The world went on walking
While the couple were one.

Your man with the camera
Feels sorry for me.
He misses the fact
That some of you see.
Your eyes are aloft
With wonder above;
Forgetting how often
We benches held love.

February, 2005

Now the Light

I was listening for the sounds that hide in the light.

Even there in the *dark* I heard the music that makes *it* bright.

I turned at once to look, to find the notes that took

Me by surprise.

In the stillness, Time, the cutpurse, is snatching up the *now*.

He will steal the moment, with its music, if we allow

His unchecked guise.

In every act, in every *thing* there is a song.

Look carefully with your ears and listen with your heart

Loving the *things* to words must be your part.

Words that match the music are never wrong.

Events are caught in the magic net of words.

Every human act sings notes truer than the truest birds.

It is the poet's work to find them.

He must search for rhythms in any moment's turning,

And *see* in the sounds, a hidden heart's unspoken yearning.

It is his work to bind them

With tender words of steel, or quiet words that feel;

Before the magic stops and Time's dark curtain drops.

LoveAtLast

I heard through the words,

I *saw* through the words,

      To something no longer mine.

Like a flock it was of a thousand birds.

And though my prayer rode only air,

I heard a song and the song was Thine.

    You heard me now.

        You brought me now

To where all loves abound.

Where all our words take flight with birds

On the other side of sound.

    For so long I hadn't noticed that

    Sound had stolen into my heart.

It played a music that made me fall in love with words.

Thank God I do not love them less.

    Thank God I love Him more.

        March, 2006

The Artist

I do not love (yet would not be without)
That unseen watching part of me which waits;
Which peers past pain, or love; past tears or doubt,
And from the clay, in leaning light creates

Moments unsaid or seen. I would not change
The ice and silence which hides behind my tears.
I *know* my heart is warm, its arms *have* range,
For in its *seeming* cold, it holds things double-dear.

It loves the perfumed mystery of your searching eyes,
As when summer (charmed by flowers, scent and shoot)
Lifts the petals of becoming hours to its skies;
Yet like the winter, undistracted, knows the root.

      I *m u s t* do this: reshape the things I see.
      And thus uncovering you, your truth discovers me.

July, 1985

Events

events forever fall on us.
they shatter like crystal on our eyes;
going out a door,
        picking up a phone,
                tearful at a touch
they crush at a turn sometimes,
        against our hearts
                and splinter.

both
    we and they
    are wounded in the happening,
mute events surprise our eyes to seeing,
    then weep for our words.
    they lie suspended to hear our saying....

for
    all things need to know and hear their names.
but only man,
    tiny forked man,
    walks in the gift of words.

stammer then,
        stutter then,
    but love and speak the moment into meaning.

Summer Emptiness

Staring at the ground

As parched as ten years long,

With breeze not April-warm

I wonder how the blades

Of grass continue and

Grow up around the feet of men.

I ask why I'm not dry as

That blown earth that races in small

Swirling tails up the funnels of the wind.

What holds my clay so moistly

In its rhythmic place?

Does the liquid blue of sky, I wonder

Show through the lattice of

My leaves, as it does there above my head?

.....quite peacefully...

July, 1969

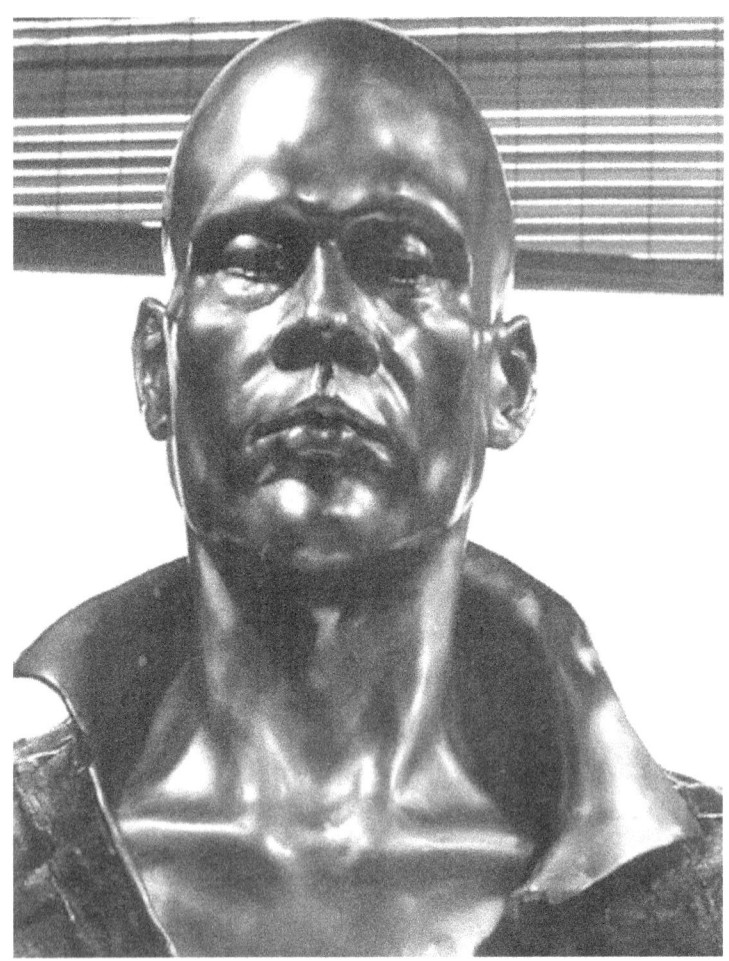

PEOPLE WHO KNEW JESUS

MARY MAGDALENE

She had heard about the paralytic whose friends had opened the roof, to get him past the crowd to this Jesus. And Jesus not only cured him but even forgave his sins. That certainly caused a stir with the Pharisees. Then there was the leper, right after that, but the thing that got her most was what He said at the dinner in Levi's house. Levi was so happy and excited when Jesus stopped at the customhouse and asked Levi to come and work with him, that he just dropped everything and left. Then he said he was going to celebrate, and asked all his fellow workers to come to his house for dinner. He asked some of the Pharisees who were nearby, but naturally most of Levi's friends were other tax-collectors. Everybody came to honor Jesus and celebrate Levi's new job. But *that* was the problem: everybody was there, all those other tax-collectors and *sinners.* When the Pharisees saw how happy Jesus was to be with them, they became quite angry and challenged Him, "Why do You eat and drink with these tax-collectors....and these *sinners?*"

But what Jesus said next, and she heard this right from one of the waiters, "It is not those who are well that need a doctor, but those who are sick. I didn't come for the virtuous but for sinners." Sinners, Mary thought. Sinners. Joy burned that word into her heart. 'What kind of man could this be?' She didn't know but He must be kind....and *forgiving.* She made up her mind, right at that moment, to follow Him and find out.

And so it was that she was one of the crowd climbing up the hill at Tabgha. There in front of her was the Centurion himself. He looked like he was helping that old woman up the grade. At the edge of the crowd they sat down together. Mary smiled to herself; like them, she thought it best to stay on the edge of things, so she found a rather large cedar and stood behind it. It wasn't very far to Magdala, so she knew her reputation there had followed her; though in fact, it wasn't very long before she had added to it in both Capernaum and Tabgha. She stayed behind the tree, even though in her heart she knew that she had changed. It had started that day she had heard He was going to be at the synagogue in Capernaum. Here was a chance to *see* Him. She slipped in with a few other women, though she always felt alone; they went up into that little balcony that was reserved for women only. But she got caught up in the excitement when they all saw Him curing that man with the withered hand. She had seen that man and noticed his hand any number of times; it always looked so shriveled. Like the others, she was leaning over the rail, straining to see, when Jesus looked up. She suddenly felt He was looking just at *her.* The look went through her. She felt so different; what was happening to her? Oh no, He was still looking at her.

She felt that she would never forget the eyes. That blue, bluer than the sky that surrounded His white robes there on the hill as He turned to the crowd. And now again she saw the eyes. Then He began to speak. *"Blessed....happy are the poor in spirit, theirs is the kingdom of heaven....Blessed are the meek...those that mourn....those that are merciful.....Blessed are the pure of heart, they shall see God....... the peacemakers...."* But Mary had stopped listening. She kept hearing, *"Happy, blessed, are the pure in heart..."* Oh, how she would love to be happy....to be pure? She was beginning to feel somewhat crushed. But something in His voice, in His eyes....the *way* He said it seemed to make it possible. Not just being happy, but *pure.* Something was happening to her, *in* her. She had gone so far into herself that she didn't even notice the crowd leaving. She hadn't seen the Centurion leaving before the rest.

The first thing she became aware of were the leaves against her bare feet; then that her body had slipped down along the bark, to the ground. She was sitting and staring at the leaves and thinking about purity. *She* was thinking about *purity.* She had mocked it for so many years. But now *"happy... blessed...shall see God."* Could this really be? Could *she* be happy? What would it be like to *see God?* She sat transfixed till the sun had gone down. She couldn't see the leaves anymore..... only those words. She finally roused herself, pulled herself up. It had begun to rain. So she headed back to her somewhat over-decorated house. Again she felt so alone; she just wanted to get inside the house.

But when she was inside she looked around rather sadly....it was so gaudy. She had never noticed that before.

It was the greatness of Magdalene to finally see and, see clearly, that she could exist no longer by herself. His eyes did that. She now knew that she carried herself like an echo down a long corridor toward oblivion. But essential to her 'greatness' was the appearance of Jesus at the height of this awareness (or perhaps *causing* it) striking in her the deepest womanly intuition she would ever have: that *here* was her completion, *here* was her means of return.... Here in Christ, in the white excitement of His passing by, was a heart that did not, *would* not, seek to use her as all the others, whose secret nights had ended with the payment of a price. Here at last she could forget those nights, whose darkness made her heart a tomb of paid-up lovers: where love had slipped the balance into lust and clawed men's souls and left them *less* after sifting out the whispered pleasure of some stranger.

She twisted on the bed where she had thrown herself. This kind of forgetting is never easy, for it is the *same* night in which she now lay down to sleep.....the same stillness that once was loud with pleasure, now festered in her till it pumped pain to every corner of remorse. The beat of the rain on her windswept roof kept telling her she was not clean and that no water could wash away her filth. The strong aroma of quince outside her window reminded her of a fragrance she had often worn and defiled.... The touch of the pillow against her face....but no, she could think no longer. She could not bear the weight of memory, and crushed with pain, the night was filled with sobbing. Her pillow was wet with tears for sin was bleeding through her eyes....and healing had begun. She hurt so badly; yet couldn't comprehend that remorse is not compunction and compunction is the sinner's hope of life. It is found by remembering, but Mary discovered it was taking her further back than sin......further back than pain....to a time when thoughts were white...when all her warring passions still slept...when all the growing forces played at the water's edge through the wide and untouched fingers of a child.

Remorse is the reaction to the ugliness of sin; compunction is the grief of having offended innocence. It is not ultimately found by looking *in*, for the soul then has lost its innocence. It is found by looking *out*, to an innocence that was passing by. And that's how Mary found it. She saw it passing by in Christ, Who *is* innocence. It takes courage to look up from self-disgust into the Face of Innocence.....courage and belief.

If we can speak of God's taking pride in anything, it is in His mercy. This is part of what Jesus came to prove........*"that though your sins are red as scarlet, or bright as crimson, they shall be made white as snow.....the bent reed I shall not break...the smoking flax..."* She had heard these words often enough to remember that she had no longer believed them...that she had in fact mocked them. Then something inside her told her that after sorrow and compunction, there must be some kind of reparation. But when love is wounded, she thought...only love can heal....reparation.... love...yes, she said and finally began to sleep. *" I will..."* trailed her eyelids softly until the dark and silence were one.

In the morning the word *'reparation'* still hung in her ears, and when she opened her eyes, there it was across the rising sun like the challenging look of someone who cares.

When she went outside she got the same scathing self-righteous looks and the winks, but she ignored them both. She stopped at the well for a drink of fresh water. She was swallowing it when she heard that Simon, the Pharisee, had invited Jesus to supper at Simon's home. She couldn't believe her ears. Jesus was going to be there. Who could stop her now? Love was going to be there.

Then she tried to think of different ruses to get into the dinner, but suddenly stopped, "No. Just go in."

"No." Again she said to herself, I need to take something in with me. She ran back to her house, gave a withering look to a man waiting by her door. "Get out of here," she virtually hissed. Startled, shocked, certainly confused, he pulled his shawl up about his face again and left. Mary ran inside the house and just then remembered this beautiful jar of really expensive nard. *That's* what she would bring. She sat on the side of her bed trying to imagine what would happen; then for a few seconds *afraid* of what could happen. She no longer could care less about the reactions of the other guests. Some of them she already knew. But what would Jesus say? The hours dragged on and so did her anxiety, but she was determined. Finally, the sun that had flamed into her room that morning had become no more than a gentle glow. She stood up, didn't bother wrapping the nard, threw her hair back and set out for Simon's.

It was darker when she got there. She could see the candles and the torches and even hear the laughter at some distance. Her steps slowed a bit; she actually stopped, almost turned. But then she looked down at herself for a moment, looked back to the lights and the laughter, lifted her head and almost strode toward the door.

When she got to the door she felt something break in her, and again was afraid. But somehow she knew that the thing in her that broke, *should* be broken. Now somewhat bent, she went through the doorway and headed straight for Jesus. There were some outraged faces and some embarrassed faces, the ones she knew, and who knew her. But there were no indifferent faces. The look of Jesus was quiet and warm. She threw herself down on her knees. The room became deathly still except for her sobbing. Her tears began to fall on the feet of Jesus making marks like raindrops in the dust still caked on His feet from the road. The tears were as bountiful as her sorrow. She took some of the hair that had fallen down over her face and began to wipe His feet. But as she touched Jesus there was an audible gasp in the room. When she kissed them, the gasp became sharper as though someone had wounded the sound itself. Mary just kissed them again and then began to anoint them with her priceless nard. Its aroma almost silenced the gasps. Simon's face had a most shocked, even wounded expression. The guests were beginning to turn toward Simon to see what he would do. But Jesus knew what Simon was thinking, what his look expressed: "If He were really a prophet He would know that a prostitute was touching, even kissing His feet. He would certainly have shunted her away." But Jesus said very simply to him, "Simon, I have something to say to you."

"Speak, Master."

"There was once a creditor who had two men in his debt; one owed him 500 denarii and the other 50. They were unable to pay so he forgave them the debts. Which of them will love him more?"

"The one who was pardoned more, I suppose." Mary froze to hear what Jesus would say.

"You are right." Then Jesus turned to Mary. *"Simon, do you see this woman?"* See her? Nobody in the room had been able to take their eyes off her since she came in. Then Jesus said,

"I came into your house and you poured no water over my feet, but she has poured out her tears over my feet and wiped them with her hair." Mary just barely dared to lift her head. *"You gave me no kiss, but she has been covering my feet with kisses since she came in."* At these words she turned her tear-filled eyes to Jesus, *"You did not anoint my head with oil but she has anointed my feet with precious nard."* Mary instinctively felt for the jar and smiled the deepest smile because the jar was empty. *"For this reason, I tell you that her sins, her many sins, must have been forgiven her or she would not have shown such great love. It is the man who is forgiven little who loves little."* Then Jesus turned to Mary and said with all the simplicity her heart could bear, *"Your sins are forgiven."*

There was that gasp again, only this time it was peppered with *Blasphemy......blasphemy! No one can forgive sin but God.* Jesus very simply, with a quiet, even voice, said to Mary, *"Your faith has saved you. Go in peace."* There was something in the way He had said, 'Your faith' that changed the silence in the room to anger. Mary kissed the feet again and then got up, and started to back away from Jesus with a thousand "Thank Yous".....She mostly bowed but she couldn't resist looking into His eyes again. All the way home her *peace* cut through the darkness for her like a torch. When she got inside the house she laughed at the decorations, knew she would change them and threw herself onto the bed. She lay there for a while happy to the point of laughing. Though even as she laughed she felt the tears fall backward from the corners of her eyes till they touched her ears. The last thing she saw before falling off to sleep were His eyes. The last word she heard was *"peace."*

When morning came there was only sunlight in her room. The glow was different. She thought she would leap out of bed she was so happy, but she just lay there smiling, trying to absorb the riches of the night that had just passed. When she finally got up and washed cleaner than she could ever remember, she sat back in her favorite chair and again started to laugh. But the mood was broken by a knock on her door. She opened it and suddenly grew very weak in her knees. There was His mother, Mary, standing in light outside *her* door. Speechless, she backed up into the room, in fact, into the same chair. She just stared as Mary stepped out of the sunlight into the house. Mary had the warmest, gentlest smile as she took a seat by the window. Then she deepened her smile at the speechless host, but before she could say anything, Mary blurted out, " *He has your eyes. Jesus has your eyes. Oh, I'm sorry to just blurt that out at you, but the blue...."*

The Mother of Jesus deepened her smile even more, but then simply said, *"Mary, you must come with us. You would be of such great help to us. He was very moved by your faith."*

"Come with you? Help you...?
"Yes, Mary, come with us.

Mary did. The two women became wonderful friends from that first day.

So Mary, like Peter and Andrew, John and James, left her home to help take care of Jesus and the men they called Apostles. It wasn't long after the mother of Jesus had come to her house that they all started out for a preaching and teaching tour to any number of towns and villages. But that first morning, when she met the Apostles for the first time, she felt very much intimidated. By now she had heard so much about them, about how much they loved Jesus, how close they were to Him. She was surprised that Susanna, the wife of one of Herod's stewards was along with them. Later Mary would see how important Susanna was for getting provisions for the group.

She couldn't help noticing how Jesus took special care of the Apostles, always explaining things to them. They didn't always seem to understand. She herself didn't understand, especially that day when Jesus had gone ahead to preach. There was a very large crowd listening to Him. Mary and the others weren't sure where they were to meet that evening, so they sidled in through the crowd to the door where Jesus was. They couldn't get in because of the press of people, so they had one of the crowd push his way up to where Jesus was to let Him know that they were out there trying to talk to Him. She was able to get within earshot and when the man told Jesus His mother and brethren were outside, Jesus said, *"Who are my Mother and my brothers?"* Mary was shocked, and speechless. *"Those who hear My word and keep it…they are my Mother and my brothers."* Mary never understood how Jesus could say such a thing. She just turned to His Mother in wonderment and confusion. But as she looked, she could see that His Mother understood.

Mary, since leaving Magdala spent the rest of her life caring for Jesus and His Apostles in their endless tours of teaching. Now and again, but rarely, she would have to be away; but never so often or so long that the Master would be out of her thoughts or prayers. Nothing about Jesus amazed her any more. She came to accept and love whatever His mystery was. Even when, after a terrible night of storms over the lake and the Apostles made it back to their house, they told her how terrified they were and that Jesus, who was sleeping, woke to their cries, gave them a kind of sad look, turned to the wind, and said, *"Be calm."* And the wind stopped, the rain let up and the lake went still. But clearly they were still shaken.

But toward the end she began to notice how upset Peter was becoming.

Jesus had told Peter something and Peter was not the same after that. He shared it with John. They always shared everything together anyhow, but this was upsetting. Actually all of them had been told but Peter and John seemed most bothered by it. It was coming up to the time for the Feast of Tabernacles and Jesus said they were going up to Jerusalem. They all thought that that was dangerous and tried to prevail against it, but Jesus insisted. At one point He even called Peter a 'Satan' and told him to get away. He *was* going up. Peter was actually a good sleeper, once he lay down, that was it. But now that he knew what could happen to Jesus in Jerusalem, all he could do was twist and turn whenever he tried to sleep. She could hear him cry out sometimes at night. She even went a couple of times to see if he was all right. When she peeked in, in his sleep Peter looked afraid.

When they got to Jerusalem Mary figured they all must have been wrong. They actually had a parade for Him, "Hosannas," palm branches, people all cheering and singing. It seemed great. The people all looked like they wanted to make Him a king. Still the Apostles seemed tense. Peter especially jumpy; John as always was the calmest one; but they all tried to stay together. Safety as a group. It was just Judas who seemed to have some work to do. He'd be gone a few hours at a time. Nobody minded since he frequently had to go out to make preparation for one thing or another. In fact, they all thought him quite brave, all but maybe John. It was funny to her, since John usually trusted everyone.

On Thursday night all the men went with Jesus, well actually all the *Apostles* went with Him for a special supper, maybe a Seder. They were pretty secretive about it. The women, with Mary His Mother, stayed together and worried. They prayed because there was something in the air. They kept watching the room, the one they had gotten from the disciple of Jesus, to see when they would be finished. Finally Susanna said, *"Relax, what could happen?"* She was standing by the window still watching and suddenly, *"Look, I told you they must be almost finished. There's Judas coming out now."* She paused as Mary got to the window, *"He must have something to do. He's not coming this way."* But there was no one else following. There was silence for what seemed hours, and now very worried looks, though they didn't know why they were upset.

Finally they saw Jesus come out followed by Peter and James and John. Then all the other Apostles, close on the heels of Jesus and Peter and John and James. They were all heading up toward Gethsemane, which seemed normal enough. Jesus often used the garden to rest and pray. But it did seem odd at this hour. What could they want in a garden? After more than an hour, Mary Magdalene said, *"I can't take this any longer. Something must have happened to them. I'm going up there."* Before she left she went over to His mother to embrace and hopefully reassure her. When she looked up she had a very different expression on her face and her hands were so cold. Mary headed out the East Gate toward the Olive Grove at the foot of the Mount of Olives. Crossing the brook of Kedron everything seemed quiet enough. She could see the three Apostles. They looked like they were asleep. Jesus had just turned to them to say something. They looked startled and finally were getting to their feet. Whatever He said to them then made them bolt upright and look towards a small group of soldiers and what looked like some synagogue elders. Mary's heart was racing and when she saw them all heading for Jesus, she could hardly breathe. She wanted to scream or yell, *something*, but Jesus looked so calm. Then she relaxed. Judas was with them. It must be all right, One of His own Apostles was with them.

Ah good, he's going over to embrace Jesus. See, he kissed Him. Mary hadn't even taken a full breath. The Name 'Jesus' virtually choked in her throat. She somehow was trying to call out. But before the words would come she saw the soldiers grab the arms of Jesus. It was all happening so fast, yet in her mind it was like the whole thing was happening in molasses, slow and awful. Peter grabbed a sword from someplace and swiped at the second soldier's head. It sheared off his ear. Before other soldiers could even take hold of Peter, Jesus had turned to him. You could see Jesus was telling him to put down the sword. Then Jesus reached to the wounded soldier, touched the side of his bleeding head, and healed him. John tried to get as close to Jesus as he could but the soldiers pushed him away. She could see Judas slipping off into the dark under the cover of one of those huge olive trees. *"O God, Judas what have you done?"* Mary fell back against a cedar and felt herself slipping down to the ground, the way she had done the first time she heard Jesus speak... or saw His eyes.

They were taking Jesus away now. Peter and John and James were still struggling and protesting. The other Apostles had fled, but some more people from the synagogue were adding to the crowd and shouting for agreement with the soldiers. The Apostles started pushing their way through the crowd to follow after Jesus. But then Peter and James seemed to hold back in some kind of confusion. John just plowed ahead. Mary got up and just stood there, frozen in amazement, with tears running down her cheeks, sobbing, until she thought of His Mother, Mary. She spun around and started back through the gate running as fast as she could to get to Mary.

"O Jesus, Your poor Mother." she said a hundred times before getting to the house. When she got there she didn't, at first, have the courage to go in. But Susanna had been at the window the whole time and now here in front of her, were Susanna and the Mother of Jesus. She tried not to blurt it out, she tried not to sob it out, without much success. His Mother gently calmed her till the story was told. Susanna slid down onto a bench. Mary fell into His Mother's arms. Mary didn't remember Simeon's words of so many years ago: *"...That a sword shall pierce your heart."* But they were there, and they were fulfilling the prophecy.

All of the events inherent in that and the many other prophecies were enacted with Divine scrupulosity. All the I's of Redemption were dotted and every T was crossed. Even the one Jesus was hung on. And when it all was over and the carried Cross was now splattered red and down; when Barabbas was free, unmindful of what his freedom cost; when even the clotted scourging with its flesh-tearing snap of lead-embedded thongs was not enough to satisfy the insatiable blood-lust of a mob, no longer men; when betrayal had exacted its suicidal price and tears had washed away the ignoble stain of cowardice, when at last the hill called Calvary was silent again, that day we have come to call Good, that Friday was ended. The Son was gone.

But Mary, out of whom seven devils had been driven, stronger and truer than all the men but John, stayed at the cross and like her first encounter knelt to kiss His feet, and kissed them now, all the while helping a Mother hold the blood-soaked Body of her Son. It had been a day of testaments to love. Love Itself was crucified but it spilled on any heart brave enough to keep open and stay near. Mary, and the Beloved Disciple, John, holding the Mother, now emptied of her tears, were as near as hearts can be. Love rained on them till all they knew was Love.

It was this Mary, her eyes and heart as empty as His Mother's, who with another Mary and Salome, went to the tomb, before the sun came up, only to find it as empty as her heart. Confused, beyond any fear, she dropped the nard and ointments when they suddenly saw a man in white who said, *"You are looking for Jesus of Nazareth, who was crucified. He is risen, He is not here. See, here is the place where they laid Him."* When Mary looked down she saw that the broken jars of ointment and of nard had spilled across the very heart of the stone.

But He was gone.

"Someone must have taken His Body," she immediately thought. *"THEY have stolen His Body."* Looking at James' mother and Salome, she cried, *"We must go and tell Peter and the rest of them."* All

three started towards the entrance to the tomb. Outside they began running together, but Mary, frantic at His disappearance, saw a gardener standing right outside the tomb. *"Sir, if you have taken Him. Tell me where you have put Him. I will go and take Him."*

Suddenly everything stopped. The whole world stopped. She heard the 'Gardener' with an unforgettable voice say, *"Mary."* All the world was in that voice; it all was new again. It was her Jesus saying her name.

"Rabboni," she cried, and as always reached down to kiss His feet.

"Do not touch me because I have not yet ascended to My Father, but go now and tell the brethren I am ascending to My Father and your Father….to My God and your God."

She immediately ran back to tell the others. They, like ourselves, found it hard to believe. They may have been slow, but Mary, in her very open heart, caressed her name and the voice that said it.

Standing, O so still in the middle of that upper room, while all the rest ran to the tomb to see for themselves, Mary from Magdala heard again in her heart a 'Gardener' gently say her name, and she knew.

November, 2005

Simon of Cyrene

                                            While
Pilate's useless gesture was running like
a sore, he turned his boneless back on Christ.
And Caesar's justice, proudest boast of Rome,
went weeping through the streets of Palestine,
until a three-day grave exploded and gave her
back her name.

          Oh in the redness of that hour,
weakness, pain and sorrow bent Him like
a reed and pulled His will until the weight
of wounds had crushed Him to the dust that clotted
where He fell....(Divine Justice seemed here
too weak in its demand of utter expiation).
And Simon, who was coming from the country
could not have been aware Whose touch it was
that caught him from the crowd and thrust him, though
he would not, to follow in a filthy work he could
not understand. Blows struck at Christ, that missed
their mark in over-anxiousness, fell hard upon
his face and shoulders. He cursed. He spat.
He swore at Christ whose inconvenient journey
with a cross had robbed him of the quiet fortune
of indifference and the ugly freedom of being
small.

          What changed him then? What force
or motion gave that turning to his will? What
warmth dispelled the winter in his heart, that in
the time since then, his name, like that of another Simon should pass
our lips in blessing when *both*
began that day in gross denial?

            Scripture leaves
the fact in silence and Time has only told us that
he turned. Could it have been the sight of frail Veronica,
whose pity blinded her to threats;
whose love had clothed her like a lion until
she could no longer bear His hurt and with
a tiny towel touched eternity; wiped Its bleeding
Face; felt its love run through her like
an endless spring, and stood there weeping when
He passed; owning a peace that she had never owned
before and a Face that she would never lose!
Could this sight of slender love have found
its way much deeper than merely Simon's eye?
Or was it pity pulled him down to find the
crawling Christ? Had he learned the secret of
Veronica and held *his soul* as veil to soothe
the swelling Face of God? And had that swollen
Countenance, that left itself upon her towel,
Burned the Image of its love, like a brand,
upon his soul?

            These things are lost in the tired
drift of stars and we can only guess while
sifting through the mounds of months and years.
They tell us sorrow changed and grew in him
until it split upon the broken, fallen Christ.
They tell us that his feet, which first had sought
so much to flee, were ripped and bruised, and mixed
their blood with His, whose steps the rain
of Time would never wash away. They tell us
how his unaccustomed hands grew strong along the way;
until they struggled with a weight far heavier
than wood.....And how he must have looked from Christ
to those few women who wept Him as he went.
How his eyes were closed to let the darkness in;
to say the things he knew he saw, could not be so.

                    And when
the darkness reached its fullness in His death;
when skies were scarred with the unfurled Figure

of its God; when the work of crucifixion had been done,
whence went old Simon? What roads were his? What quiet
place would hide him while he wept the awful pictures
from his mind.

          Again the question finds no answer.
In the page where once Christ walked; Simon is a sentence
and then silence. And we can only wonder where he went.

But *w h y* he came and *w h y* his name should mark
the record of those fearful days is nearer to the
mind than first we might have guessed.

                    O, is he not
the sum and model of beginnings not our own?
Of motions fed with*out* the heart.....that first
Unfinal gross indifference of the will?

                  Simon,
you did not love him when they wrenched you
from the crowd. But sharing in a painful
labor has a way of binding hearts, a way
Of wounding wills until they bleed another's
tears. You have become a symbol, O, Simon of
Cyrene! *You* are the hope of those too young,
or weak, or small to love Him from the outset
of the task....too fearful of its weight to leave
their place among the crowd....of those who have
the backward-looking and the fear of letting go.

Then get, then grant us, the strength that made you strong!
O, Simon of Cyrene, I chant aloud your song.

The Centurion

He had just come into the city from his garrison. Very few Centurions, out-posted as he was, away even from Palestine, could feel as he could, riding through an occupied city; though it was hard to think of Capernaum as a city. Certainly as far as population went, it hardly qualified as a town. But it was important, situated almost midway between Egypt and Damascus, just off the Via Maris. Its shores wet by the low northern waves of Galilee. The town itself had a rather dark, even gloomy look, from the lava which made up most of the stone used for the buildings. It had however the most beautiful view looking south, across the usually placid Sea of Galilee. From the left, as the sun came up it did its best to lift the dinginess of the basalt houses. But it was in the evening, when the sun was almost set that fishermen, heading out for a night's work, got the loveliest view of their town. But as I say, Capernaum was important, for more then the beauty of its vistas. The Via Maris was the main trade route to Damascus, and it passed right along the northern edge of the town. And so a great deal of commerce went through its gated customhouse. And situated as Capernaum was at the northwest corner of the Sea of Galilee, it controlled about five miles of that coast. Therefore, it was important to Rome. The Centurion was stationed there, with his garrison, just east of the town to keep order and the trade route open. Rome was never careless even with its little outposts.

In fact, he had just ridden down from the Via Maris, turning off at the mile marker which always brought a kind of wry smile to his lips. The marker "VIA MARIS" was in bold *Roman* letters. It was pretty much the only Roman sign in all of Capernaum, except for his and his soldiers uniforms, and the endless banners. His red cape and silver breastplate certainly marked him as a foreigner, and since he wore a Roman uniform, it marked him as an *occupier*. Though oddly enough, the native Israelites were openly glad to see him. They remembered his daily trips into the center of town to check on the progress of *the* building. He oversaw the black basalt stones being put in place for the foundation and the walls of the synagogue. Virtually every day. *He, the Roman Centurion* had not only given permission for the building, but was making it happen. It was, of course, not one of great splendor; even its walls were of black basalt stone. The white rock of greater synagogues and temples was just not available in this little seacoast town. In fact the basalt was the ordinary material for all the houses and shops in Capernaum. They were virtually all one-story high, (except, of course, the synagogue itself which had a loft, a kind of upper story for the women.) The rest, as I say, were one-story with only a wood roof. The basalt stone was not strong enough to hold the heavier roofing tiles. The boards used instead for the roof were placed criss-cross to each other for strength and sealed with pressed mud and straw over the wood.

He remembered one day, after hearing so much about this Jesus, Who had come to stay here.... and preach, that there was such a crowd outside a house where He was preaching, and they say healing, that nobody else could fit in *or* out. And he saw four men carrying some sick person whom they said needed to see Jesus; he saw them climb up onto the roof, dig the dirt and straw away, pull a few of the boards apart and then lower their sick friend down into the house. There was momentary bedlam and then the most unusual silence. He heard some- one at the edge of the crowd whisper, "They carried him on that litter, all the way from Bethsaida." The Centurion was still struck by the silence, until a voice suddenly yelled "Blasphemy!" Then someone ran out of the house, pushing his way through the crowd and tearing at his garments. He watched him running down the street and then turned to see another man, with the crowd all pointing at him. He asked a villager if *that* was the one he saw lowered into the house. With eyes staring and mouth wide open, he finally was able to say, quietly, almost in a whisper, "Yes." Then the house emptied; the crowd poured out, half with questions, the other half with wonder, as they followed, what clearly was a wonderworker, down toward the lake.

He shook himself loose from the memory and said, "Good morning Rabbi. How is the fishing? I can see most of the boats were out last night." "Every night, Sir. But *last* night was especially good. Lots of fish. They *all* came back loaded down. They're down at the shore right now, cleaning the big ones, and salting some of the others for drying. Dry fish I don't like, but what are you going to do? By the way, I heard there is another caravan coming back from Damascus. They'll be passing here very soon. Do you think, Sir, that they'll do any trading here? Maybe to re-supply? I know they'll stop at the customs house for the tax. *Always* the tax I tell you....well better them than us. O, yes, have you found anyone else to take Levi's place? I just saw him heading down to the lake with the Nazarene. It's been quite a while since Jesus took him away from us. Somehow to take a *tax collector*; who would have thought *that, a tax collector.* Well, you never know."

"Rabbi, did you hear the excitement up at Peter's house? It reminded me of the time you told me about, when Peter's mother-in-law was so terribly sick. And again it was that Jesus who was there. The next day you told me, you saw her in the market, shopping."

"More than that, they said she got right up and fixed their supper. No doubt he's different."

The Centurion seemed to drift off for a moment, then turned and said, "Rabbi, about the tax collector, yes, we're getting one." Then he turned and rode off at an easy gallop past the synagogue up toward Peter's house. Peter's house was only a couple of hundred yards from the synagogue. But the day was pretty hot, so he dismounted and sat down on a bench outside the house. The smell of fish always hung in the air in this little fishing village, even when a cool fresh wind blew up from the south across the lake. The lake had no salt but the drying fish along the beach had their own bite. Still the smell was singularly intense right here, he thought And there, over by a barrel, were some pretty dirty nets waiting to be repaired and cleaned. They were probably Andrew's.

Everyone in the village knew where everyone else lived but Peter's house seemed, not only to be known, but also visited by just about everybody, often in pretty large numbers. The Centurion hadn't been here in Capernaum when Peter and his brother Andrew came over from Bethsaida, but he had heard a great deal about them, especially now that Jesus seemed to be staying there. It made the Centurion smile when he thought about the two fishermen. Peter and Andrew had come over from Bethsaida, apparently because of the frequent flooding there. They were tired of being up to their hips *in* water. And *here* they spend 'most every night *on* the water. Of course, it didn't hurt that the woman Peter married lived in Capernaum.

Peter and Andrew could be seen every night heading for the shore. Everyone here knew them, liked them; and *they knew* the lake. If there were fish in the deep or the shoals, any at all, their boat would come back with heavy baskets.

Then, you could see them coming back every morning, at first light heading in, to beach their wet and wooden livelihood and start the messy job of cleaning the boat, the fish and themselves.

But all that had stopped now. Jesus had seen them cleaning their nets along the beach one morning, over toward Tabgha, (the water there was warmer because of the springs, and seemed to attract more fish.) and He said quite simply, *"Come and follow me."* Actually, He had said it to Andrew, but he ran to tell Peter. And they both were gone. Then John and *his* brother heard the same words and *they* were gone. Their father, old Zebedee, was left just staring. And it wasn't too long after, that Levi, the tax collector, much to everyone's amazement, left his table and the cash, and *he* was off with the others, not so much with the others as *with Jesus*.

Jesus must have had some 'way' about Him. You don't just drop your livelihood, your boat, your nets, your very lucrative job as tax collector, living at the customhouse in the pay of Herod himself and follow someone you never even met before. But there really *was* something about Him that was different, very different. I heard Him one day. I was on my way back from Tabgha, a small village, also on the lake but a couple of miles from Capernaum. I liked going over to Tabgha, with its seven springs that made land around it so fertile. It was actually pretty lush, wide areas of grass. That's what I liked about the place: it seemed to hold the memory and the excitement of that day when Jesus fed all those people, with what seemed like nothing. But I know friends that were there and they swear they ate. There even were baskets-full left over. Somehow I'm *drawn* to the place.

But on that day coming back from Tabgha I saw a rather large crowd heading across the Via Maris and starting up the hill there. They seemed excited. Some were actually running up the hill. There were mothers carrying babies and fathers snatching up children who weren't moving quickly enough. I knew exactly what was happening: Jesus must be up there ahead of them.

I didn't want to frighten any of them, so I dismounted and tied my horse to a bush at the foot of the hill, left my cloak on the saddle and started to climb the hill. It was only about two or

214

three hundred yards high and the slope was gentle so it wasn't too hard on some of the more elderly, climbing ahead of me. I remember giving a hand to this rather tired little woman who was at first startled by the uniform, and the short sword but in the end she said she was very grateful. We both sat down at the edge of the crowd as Jesus began to stand and look out over the sea of faces. I don't know what it was that happened, either He changed as He began to speak, or I changed as I listened. But *something* happened. I never felt so peaceful, so comforted; yet I never felt so moved. I kept hearing *"Blessed.....Blessed..."* but in the strangest combinations. Then I could sense around me a peaceful...a blessed intensity. Though energy, it was an energy that fixed you in place. It didn't let you move. Whoever had there been that said before Him, on that day, overlooking peaceful Galilee that the *poor were blessed or that the meek would inherit the earth?*....Most people there never inherited anything but debts from parents whom life had out-walked and left them like victims on that road to Jericho. Then *the pure of heart would see God*.....Would I ever see God? I wondered. Most painful was my hand inching toward my sword as I heard,*"...Blessed are the peacemakers...they'll be the children of God."* I imagined to myself what a child of God must be. Suddenly I could see all the helmets and shields and swords back at the barracks clanging to the ground with a great clamor...and human cries mixed in with the clatter. Somehow the feeling of peace was still with me, but it was beginning to have an edge.

I patted the old lady I was sitting with, on her shoulder. She smiled, a kind of wan but still warm smile. I stood up, paused a bit, then found my way back to my horse.

I could never forget that day, or *that* voice, or whatever it was that happened to me.

I had sat for a good while on that bench on the shaded side of the house lost in thought and those memories. Until I, slowly at first, but then with growing attention, turned to a flurry of activity on the eastern street coming from the barracks. There were two of my men running up the street toward me. As they ran, since they seemed so intent, I noticed shutters being hurriedly shut. After all, these were Roman soldiers.

"Sir, Marcus, your aide had an accident in a tent near your headquarters. He was bleeding so badly we brought him into your rooms. We all knew how important he was to you, so they sent us running. But we couldn't find you, so we checked at the synagogue, because you sometimes go there to talk with the rabbi. Him, we found and told him, in case he saw you before us..." They were out of breath, but still the Centurion cut in.

"Accident?" he said. "What happened?"

"Sir, he was demonstrating a trick move and slipped. He fell on his sword. It cut the inside of his thigh and is bleeding badly. The doctor said that he stuffed the wound to stop the bleeding but he doesn't think it will save him."

The Centurion jumped to his feet, started toward his horse to race back to the camp, when he suddenly stopped, looked at Peter's house, thought for what seemed an eternity. He could see flashing in his mind's eye the sick man being lowered through the roof, the man freed from possession at the synagogue, the cured paralytic, Peter's mother-in-law, but mostly the *voice* on the hillside. The authority and the kindness he heard in that voice. He turned and started instead toward the beach. He had barely taken one step when he thought of how unworthy he was to actually go face to face with such a holy man. At that moment the rabbi was coming out of the synagogue. The Centurion called to him, "Rabbi, my friend, I need your help. You are a holy man. My aide had an accident. He's badly hurt…dying maybe… He has been with me for years, six or seven campaigns….never any place but by my side….Will you go to Jesus? For me. He's at the water's edge. He *can*…I know He *will* help me…"

"Oh, I'm so sorry for your aide. But true, He *will* help. I will tell Him how much you have helped His people. How much you have helped *us*…You built our synagogue. Come let us go together to ask Him."

"O, no Rabbi. *You* must go. I am not worthy. I am not even a Jew."

So the rabbi took off with all the haste his years would allow. Fortunately Jesus had finished speaking at the shore and had started up from the beach. Another elder had joined the rabbi. They hurriedly told Jesus about the Centurion and his dying friend. Then they earnestly tried to explain why Jesus should help. "He is friendly towards our people, in fact, he's the one who built our synagogue." Jesus smiled gently and said "Take me to his house.

When the Centurion could see that Jesus was actually going to come to his house, he could hear in his mind the *voice,* and the words, *"…pure of heart…."* and *"..Peacemaker…."* and how cold the hilt of his sword felt on his hand that day. He felt the flush in his face and said to one of his soldiers still standing by, "Go to Him and tell Him not to trouble Himself. I am not worthy that He should come under my roof. Tell Him that is why I didn't presume to come to Him myself. Let Him just say the word and my friend will be healed. For I too am a man subject to authority. I have soldiers under me. I say to one 'Go' and he goes; to another, 'Do this.' And he does it." He said the words in the familiar tone of an 'order' but there was something in his heart like fear; yet not like any fear he had ever felt. It was more like the strange fear of *disappointing*. But who?

As the soldier ran to give the message he couldn't help smiling to himself at the irony of actually acting out what his message said. When Jesus heard the words, He was astounded at the faith and the man. He turned to those following Him and said, "I tell you, not even in Israel have I found faith like this." Then Jesus called to the Centurion and said, "Go back then, you have believed; so let this be done for you." It was then, for the first time that the eyes of the Centurion met the eyes of Jesus, and he was happy that hearts have words.

By the time the Centurion got back to his horse and for a while stood quietly trying to absorb the wonder of the eyes he had just seen, there was another pair of his soldiers racing up the same street, but this pair had faces glowing. They shouted from the length of the street, "Commander, Sir, Marcus is fine. You won't believe it, but he's up and about, as if nothing had happened.

But the Centurion *did* believe it. He wondered more though: how many *others* would? Indeed, a lot had happened.

For the rest of *his* life, the eyes had happened.

November, 2005

Old Simeon

Old Simeon had reached an age which startled his friends, but in his heart he felt life only began when he saw, one winter's day, a young woman with her almost luminescent Child come into the temple precincts, out of the very cold February frost. She had come, fulfilling the law, to present her male child to God. Suddenly he felt that all of those years were meant for this moment of gift: when he could lay his hands on the head of this shining Boy; and then take Him into his arms. Simeon probably didn't feel the Spirit coursing through his cells, but he spoke the words. The longed for Consolation of Israel was there somehow in the eyes of this Boy. The years of prayer were now answered; the prophets and their promise had been fulfilled. He was looking into the clear infant eyes of Hope. He could at last say to God, "Now you can dismiss your servant, O Lord, in peace, for my eyes have seen our salvation."

His few minutes of fame had begun with, "There was a man in Jerusalem whose name was Simeon….." (not very noteworthy) but the words he spoke that day are said over and over, a thousand times by every priest. "Now you can dismiss your servant, O Lord"……Simeon had walked into Scripture for the length of a paragraph, yet all of us still know his name.

He had met and recognized the future Christ, and from his mouth came the shape of this Boy's mission, with an appalling footnote about the Child's mother. "A sword would pierce her heart…" Simeon had waited all his life to say these words. Then like Anna, a prophetess from the tribe of Asher, he stepped out of time and slipped back into distance and the dark, and then was heard no more.

He had done all the Father wanted him to; it was enough.

How many of us walk along the edge of Sacred Scripture, unknown, secure in our own obscurity, but also peering into these events, hoping to hear their echo in our own hearts? Even dreaming in their shadows what **we** *might have been*, only to discover that facts are better then dreams. Coming to understand finally that **WHO** we are, is what *we* made, **but not alone. His hand was always in us.** *Who we are* comes from *our* clay and *His* grace; and always: how responsive we were to the Potter's hand.

Judas

        His weight upon the waves is washed and
                                      Gone.
Oh, is this the night "my soul, my daughter....
                                CRY!"
On the silver banks of sands,
                    Among the hippos, where the trees
Are big as Kings......
            But look! The ladder is melted,
                              The traffic is air.
There, where I would not cross
The gifts they bore were wounds.....
        I had heard the rumor in my flesh,
There would be a kiss...
My blistered blood has told me....the loss
Is clear. There are no tunes
                Of Glory
         Done...unto
                  Remission....?
The rope......unlidded the tears.....and
                            The dark.

                                      December, 1969

Peter on the Lake

We were rowing on Galilee when someone thought he heard footsteps. It must have been John who caught it first. He always could hear more and see farther than the rest of us. But mostly he just watched.

Ghosts don't splash, and yet that light, that silhouette of white must have felt the wet and spray across his feet. We were never afraid in the boats before, but we never saw anything like this either. John said with eyes wider than his gaping lips, "I think it is the Lord." The oars by now had steadied the boat; still Peter's leaping to his feet almost capsized us. Then to the wonderment of all he called in a hoarse, almost thrusting whisper, "Lord, if it is You, call me and I'll come." Even in our terror of the sight, the rest of us looked with ill-concealed scorn at the rash and blustering Peter. He never felt it, for his eyes were fixed. Then above the wind and the white splashing of the waves, they heard: "Come." Peter didn't fumble or look at the rest of us for support; he virtually vaulted over the side, but no splash. You'd think it was a floor he was standing on, the way he landed. He didn't even look down, just away, toward the Voice and the Light. But now *we* almost capsized, with each of us leaning, straining to be able to see, to watch what would happen. All slack-jawed we sucked the wonder and the night into our lungs; but there he was standing, just out of reach; his eyes glued to the Voice. Then without hesitation, as though he had left all of his fear in the boat with us, Peter started to walk. He was on water and he was *walking.* Step by step he moved to....the Lord. John was right: it *was* the Lord. Peter wasn't in any kind of mad trance, though he kept his eyes fixed; but were *we?*

We all just stared; we didn't dare look at each other, just stared. I could feel Matthew's breath on my neck. It was warm and wet but somehow it made me cold. It was so unlike the whole rest of the night; we could feel the cold and the wet but something in *us* began to burn. Now I dared to look at John and he seemed just to glow. I could see the fright in his face, but it had begun to melt. I swung my eyes back to Peter with his fixed eyes. His steps seemed to slow; he was becoming more cautious. Jesus still beckoned and waited. Then I could see His eyes were fixed; first on Peter then on all of us. He watched, but not measuring, not like a test or anything. *That* was where the burning was from; it seemed to run down His waiting arms. Peter paused for a moment, could see the arms, and took four, maybe five quick strong steps, almost strides.

Then suddenly he stopped. The wind blew his hair into his eyes; for a second he blinked. The wind came up with greater gusts. His cloak began to billow like our sail. We all instinctively *looked* at our sails. They were filling; the boat lurched. Then as one, we swung back to Peter. Water was up past his ankles and he looked down. Fear flung his arms out and he began to sink. He could swim, but he began to sink, not only into the waves but under his fear. I suddenly wanted to yell: "You can do it, Peter!" But all I could do was to cling more tightly to the boat. I could feel my body, which had been so tense, slowly relax and I slid back onto the seat. Jesus had taken a step toward Peter and now He was, almost kneeling on the water, reaching for Peter. I could hear in my head those words "I will make you fishers of men." And right here, in the middle of this unimagined moment, He was showing us *how.* Someone should count the ironies.

Then Peter soaking, with his black hair still running down his terrified face, as though the night were in tears, felt the Hand of Jesus, clasping his. The terror left his face only to be replaced by an unfathoming anguish at the words, "You of little faith." The terror left all of us and we shared the anguish; thinking, but far from words: What could He want? What kind of faith, or what *depth* of faith would be enough?

We all tried to help Peter get back into the boat, but no matter how we pulled and tugged at him and his wet robes, he kept struggling to free his face from the cloth and strained to set his eyes on Jesus. Perhaps it was Genesareth running from his eyes, but they seemed more like tears. Jesus watched all this with some strange warmth in His look and stepped easily into the boat. No one spoke but some of us remembered that night He slept through the storm and upbraided us for being afraid. Should we now have remembered and should our hearts have known? Was there disappointment in the smile with which the eyes of Jesus had just embraced us all? We knew that smile and how many times it was edged with a friend's pain. It seems to be part of being friends.

By now we all were looking expectantly at the Lord, but now there was only warmth in His so-clear eyes. Whatever disappointment there was, He kept in His heart. We just looked and wondered when we'd learn.

Bartimaeus

I am Bartimaeus and I am blind. My father said I must have *done* something, for God to punish me this way. But some of my neighbors, when I was young, when I *had* neighbors, said, "It was probably your father's sin that did this." I don't know why they would say that about him, because he was never even unkind to me. Once I heard him weeping. He didn't know how well my ears could see; so I never told him that I heard. But still, we were so poor and I was just another mouth to feed. I thought if I go out and beg, maybe I could help them that way. But you know, it's amazing: everybody seemed to agree. *If you were blind, even **born** blind, you must have deserved it.* It was almost as though, if they helped you, it would be like offending God's justice or something. Whatever it was, very few people threw me anything.

But then some friends said that the people up around Jericho were kinder, nicer or something. I didn't see any reason they should be; but there certainly was nothing here. So I said, "Why not?" The worst they can do is ignore me, like here. But where's Jericho? Again, another friend said he was heading in that direction; he'd take me so far, and then I'd have to fend for myself. The next day we set out. Aside from some scrapes and bumps and people laughing when I stumbled, it wasn't so bad. About half-way there my friend began to sound upset and I knew he was about to leave me. "Now I've heard that there are thieves along this stretch, so watch ou...." Then he caught himself; so we both laughed. He was going to tell a blind man to watch out.

The rest of the way wasn't so bad. There were some more warnings about thieves, but I wasn't bothered. I wasn't *helped* too much either; but I wasn't bothered. Then I met a rabbi who told me about this Great Rabbi who had cured some blind people. One of them was at the pool near Siloam. "Damn, why didn't *I stay* there? I was there for almost a week." Later the rabbi made a fire; he was really very kind. But all I could think about was, "Siloam....and maybe someday..." The night had a chill, but what's a chill when you can't see? Still I sidled closer to the fire. When morning came the rabbi was gone. So off again I went; it was only a short way now. "There I'll find some place to sit and..." then I could feel my lips curl – as I said, almost aloud to myself.... "and *hope*."

I heard some footsteps, sounded like a woman; she paused for a moment, mumbled something and suddenly I felt something fairly heavy land in my lap. My legs were criss-crossed to make like a basket. I could feel and smell the bread. Thank God. That was all for that day; but it tasted so good.

The next day, in fact the next few days, were hot in the sun and cold at night. But you wouldn't believe it; a few people stopped and dropped a coin now, another coin then. Strange nobody said anything. After I had five or six coins I asked this man – he had a kind voice – what the coins were. He said four were denarii and one was....He leaned over and whispered, "Put *that one,* the bigger one away. Hide it. It's silver." I couldn't believe it. I was beginning to feel rich. It will last me weeks. So much for coins, but then two apples, an orange and some grapes. And, of course, the few crumbs from my bread. "My friend was right about Jericho. It's like heaven." The day wore on; the night came; the cold came; but morning seemed different, not hot, just a different kind of warmth.

There was a lot of bustle and voices; a crowd was coming; then I heard it: *that Name....* Somebody said "Lord," I asked whom? *"Jesus,"* they said.

"The Rabbi, from the pool at Siloam. Who cured that blind man?" "Yes, you fool. Get out of the way." *"The Nazarene?"*

"Jesus, Son of David, have pity on me!" A couple of men's voices told me to shut up. But louder than before, **"SON OF DAVID, HAVE PITY ON ME!"**

Jesus stopped; He turned in the direction of the cry. Everyone went silent. Then Jesus said, *"Come here. Bring him here."*

When I heard that, I leapt to my feet. Everything in my lap, all I owned went flying: the crumbs, the coins, the apples, the oranges. I hadn't seen them before; I certainly didn't see them now. They all were gone now, even the silver coin I had hidden in my beat-up and filthy tunic. I bolted from the helping hands, stumbling, tripping, bouncing off bystanders. Some of those following started to laugh; I certainly was a comic sight. Others stifled their laughing but couldn't help pointing at this sorry sight, tripping and stumbling toward the Voice. I'm sure I looked the fool. As Jesus turned His eyes to me, they stilled to silence every face they passed over. Now the silence was almost sacred. I, too, should have frozen in the silence, but I was too excited. *HE* was here.

"What do you want me to do for you?"
"Lord that I may see."
"Receive your sight. Your faith has saved you."

Now the silence beggared stillness. I, Bartimaeus, the blind man, opened my eyes. They were hazel and looked into the bluest pools of light I ever imagined, the eyes of Christ. Their gaze was warmer than their color; at last I knew what tenderness was. I was looking back at it, in Him. The people still hung onto the edges of this silence, waiting for 'whatever would happen.' There were people and trees and rocks and sky to see, and even the dust which was everywhere, but I couldn't take my eyes from those gentle eyes that had just given my own back to me. Then tears formed along my lashes and spilt to line my dust-caked cheeks. There was beauty there, spilt out from the quiet eyes that looked at me.

Suddenly, it was clear what had happened and the crowd erupted. "He can see, Look, he can see!" The sudden burst of joy from the crowd tore me for a moment from the Face of Christ....to the trees and the sky and cheering faces. I screamed my thanks to Yahweh, but I would never forget that the Face of Jesus was the first face I ever saw. It would be etched in my heart forever; yet for now, I turned my face again and again to Christ. This time the cheering wonder all around me broke my lips, like thunder, in cries of thanks, but my 'thanks' were never louder than my tears. Tears give the eyes their light, their sparkle and mine belonged to Christ. ANOTHER DAY I WOULD FIND THE TIME AND THE WAY TO TELL THIS STORY. For this day all I could do was join the excited crowd, calling out to anyone who would listen, "*I can see. HE did it*." Then amid the tears, "He gave me my sight." Then again I'd meet the eyes of Christ; and again, the tears would come. I almost couldn't see again, for the tears.

June, 2004

John the Baptist

It was toward evening, but the sky to the west didn't look so beautiful to John with manacles on his wrists and the chains dragging along between his legs.

He and the three guards from Herod's troops had been walking for almost five hours. It was a nine-mile trek to the fortress prison at Machaerus. None of what he heard about the place was good. He glanced at the last rays of the sun as the silhouetted fortress rose to block the sky. They got there much too quickly now; then the last bit of nature's noise was blotted out by the slamming of Machaerus' great gates. Huge, ugly, and ponderous might be better words.

He looked over his shoulder, back to the world that had just disappeared, yet there was no tightness in his gut. He regretted nothing that he had said to Herod, though the hatred in the malevolent eyes of the woman sitting next to Herod almost made him shudder, not in fear, but in disbelief that such a look was possible. But he knew he was wearing the chains she forged for him.

Whatever was happening, God had asked of him; so be it.

When they were inside, they caught the eye of some men gathered or perhaps working just to the left. One of them seeing John, nudged his friend saying, "Isn't that the one who baptizes everybody?"

"You mean whose always yelling 'Repent?' He's sure to Yahweh not going to have too much success in this place." There was a mocking defiance in the way he emphasized 'Yahweh.' John half-turned his head, but he was by now used to the mixture of mockery and awe. He certainly had many followers, most of whom were pretty confused for the last month or so. They had heard of this Jesus. Many of them had gone out to hear Him for themselves. Some even had stopped following John. It was strange that he didn't seem to mind. They still didn't know that *that* was what John wanted to happen.

But right now the guards were swinging open his cell door. It turned out to be much more of a dungeon. He fell forward into the dark as he heard the laughing of the guards with their lamps pushing the darkness aside down the corridor. Then there was silence, only silence, broken now and then by a moan, or a curse, or someone just crying out. There was one thin shaft of dirty light, which seemed to be coming from a small opening in the ceiling between the stones. By the time his eyes adjusted to the dark, he made out a pile of straw along the moss and grime-covered wall opposite the door. It stunk. Its reeking odor even stood out from the fetid stench that made up the air in the rest of his new home. He stood in the center and thought of the years in the desert.

At least, out there was breathable air, and the Lord knows, there was plenty of light. Again, if this was what Yahweh wanted, so be it.

He was accustomed to being alone. His father Zachary always told him: he was special. God had some work for him to do. In the desert he was alone, with God. They talked and talked, he and God; it was his natural way to pray, and day-by-day Yahweh's presence became more and more real, and His Voice clearer and clearer, until it became like crystal. Beautiful and chimed, but demanding. His father, old Zachary was right; he had a particular work to do. Yahweh had told him. *He was to Prepare; to preach a preparation of repentance for the Holy One of God, the Holy One that He would send.* So from that first day out of the wilderness, *that* is what he did. And *that* is what had brought him here, to Machaerus, in the middle of this darkness, covered with this inhuman stench.

He thought of his mother, how he loved her, and how it would break Elizabeth's heart to see her son in such a wretched state. And suddenly the question: was he here for having done God's will or Herodias' hatred? Had he *completed* his work of preparation, or had her hatred cut him short? He remembered that day at the Jordan, when he first saw the one called Jesus. The words, "BEHOLD THE LAMB OF GOD," still rang in his ears....in his heart. That was all so clear; even how terrified he was at the Other Voice. That Day was etched in his mind. He had been so terribly sure of what he was doing, but *was* that Jesus really the Christ? He fell to his knees, in the muck; his head falling back from his strained neck, with his eyes shut so tight they squeezed out his desperate tears. He cried out so even God could hear, "Have I done Your work? Is it finished? Did You mean that *He* is the Messiah? Lord help me. Answer me, I pray. My people are confused." John now hardly noticed the stench, or the muck, or even the dark. Quiet slowly began to return. His Lord, silent though He was, was with him. Silently he slipped to the floor, and hoped for dreams. But they didn't come. For a number of days he waited and he pleaded but the only sound was darkness.

Then one day he heard there was a mob of his followers outside the main gate, some pleading, some praying, some demanding to see him. The chief guard finally gave in, rather than have such great trouble around *his* prison. A small group was escorted down the hardly visible steps, and then to his 'cell.' They tried to call out greetings but his voice ran through their tearful words like a sword. "Is it He?" he cried. "Is Jesus the Messiah? Go ask Him, 'Is it Now?'" "Now," he shouted. "But John," they tried to interrupt. And without any comfort, for them or him, he sent them off. "Come, and tell me!" was the last thing they heard as they left the steps.

John again sank to his knees, "Thank You. Thank You, O Thank You my Lord." His arms outstretched, with some little light left in his eyes, he gradually edged through thanksgiving, into sleep. And this time there *were* dreams. In them he could hear himself shouting, "He will come after me. I am not worthy to loosen the straps of His sandals." Then Zachary stepped into the dream; he just stood there silently, but with affirming eyes. At that, John's face gave way, almost, to a smile and the muscles of his chest relaxed. He could see the faces of some followers turn toward Jesus, as he called, "Behold the Lamb...." He dreamt of the happiness of his coming out of the wilderness, preaching, preaching, "Repent," preaching.....then the faces turning toward that Man....he somehow knew he knew. Their faces, his followers' faces all open, wide-eyed and straining to hear. Maybe he *had succeeded.* The dream was warm; *he* was warm, even in the chill of these stones....even on these wet and cold stones, and that pervasive hatred, worse than the stench.....or the stones.

Eventually, that night, he could feel himself falling off to sleep, hunched against that foul smelling straw. Though he soon found out, it wasn't really sleep, his lids, though drooping, weren't totally closed. He began to make out in the shadowy shapes of darkness, someone dancing, better, some*thing* moving, gyrating. It was moving to some evil triumphant laughter. There was the soft, sudden glitter of silver bits or shimmering gold; then it went to blackness. But before he dozed off completely, he thought he saw a light; it was getting closer and closer; then finally.... again... the dark.

What he didn't know, didn't *see*, may have dreamed, was the torch not quite behind the twisted grin of Herodias peering in through the door of his cell. She, and her retinue, had come in during the day. *She* was here at Machaerus. Of course, she hadn't come alone. Herod and his willowy daughter were still in the palatial marble and ebony suites, up many flights and over to the East Wing which jutted out like a claw into the night. They were listening to servants going over the details for Herod's great gala; a celebration to end all celebration, he thought, not without some glee. He noted the number of trumpets and over a thousand candles! Musicians from as far away as Tyre and Sidon! "What about the bears for the baiting?" he asked. "A dozen."

John was startled from his sleep by first, voices in the passageway, then by the figure at the door. It was Philip. They would only let in one of the men he had sent to Jesus to find out, "Was He the Messiah?"

Philip was clearly frightened by all the soldiery that had accompanied Herod's arrival at the prison. He started immediately to tell John about the soldiers and Herod; but John quickly cut him off. ***"What did Jesus say?"*** he virtually hissed. Philip froze for a few seconds at the fierceness in John's voice. Then said, "He told us, 'Tell John what you see: The blind see; the lame walk; the deaf hear; lepers are cleansed....the poor have the gospel preached to them....and tell John, Blessed is he who is not scandalized in Me.' Then Philip excitedly said "You were right that day at the Jordan, you remember: You said 'the One over whose head the dove hovers, would come with the Spirit.' You remember?" Of course John remembered. How could he forget? But at this moment his face had changed. Tears filled his eyes. It was the last part; somehow he already knew the rest. Those last few words were Jesus talking to him. Directly to him!

And TELL JOHN: "Blessed is he who is not scandalized in Me"

Jesus was telling him He knew what was happening to him. And He cared! He smiled at those little words of comfort tacked onto the wonders Jesus proclaimed. He couldn't get out of his head:

those words were for *him. Jesus had sent those words to **him**. "Tell John not to be scandalized in me."* How could he ever be scandalized by Jesus? Every word he had ever heard about Jesus was just some different shape of Love. Yes, He **was** the Messiah. Just then, a guard grabbed Philip, smacked him with the flat side of his short sword, threatened to use the business end if he didn't move quickly enough, and chased him to the staircase, out of sight.

With some kind of peace he had never known or felt, John went over to sit and lean against the wall. He never even noticed the straw that stunk. "Jesus," he said, "Scandalized…" Tears filled his eyes, his shoulders shook and he whispered again, "O Jesus."

Now and again, in the dark, he wasn't sure, was he hearing some music, which sounded like it was a mile away. But the beat built. He thought he could distinguish different instruments. The music got louder and wilder. He now could make out shouts and clapping to the beat…almost erotic….wilder and wilder. Suddenly there was a roar, mad cheering, then the quiet of the dark returned. He relaxed against the wall until he turned his head toward the sound of footsteps, something metal scraping against a wall; then a great clank of armor stop outside his cell. The door flung open. He stayed against the wall till someone dragged him by the hair to the center of the cell; a sword against the back of his legs drove him to his knees. He knelt there a moment, somehow hearing Jesus. Then he turned his eyes to meet the glint of a torch-lit sword coming down on his neck. A few moments later, some clanging up the steps, into the great hall, and John's head was at the feast. He could no longer smell the stench; but Salome could when she handed that platter-full to her father. She felt her mother's hand at the very edge of the silver tray, as though she wanted to make sure.

July, 2004

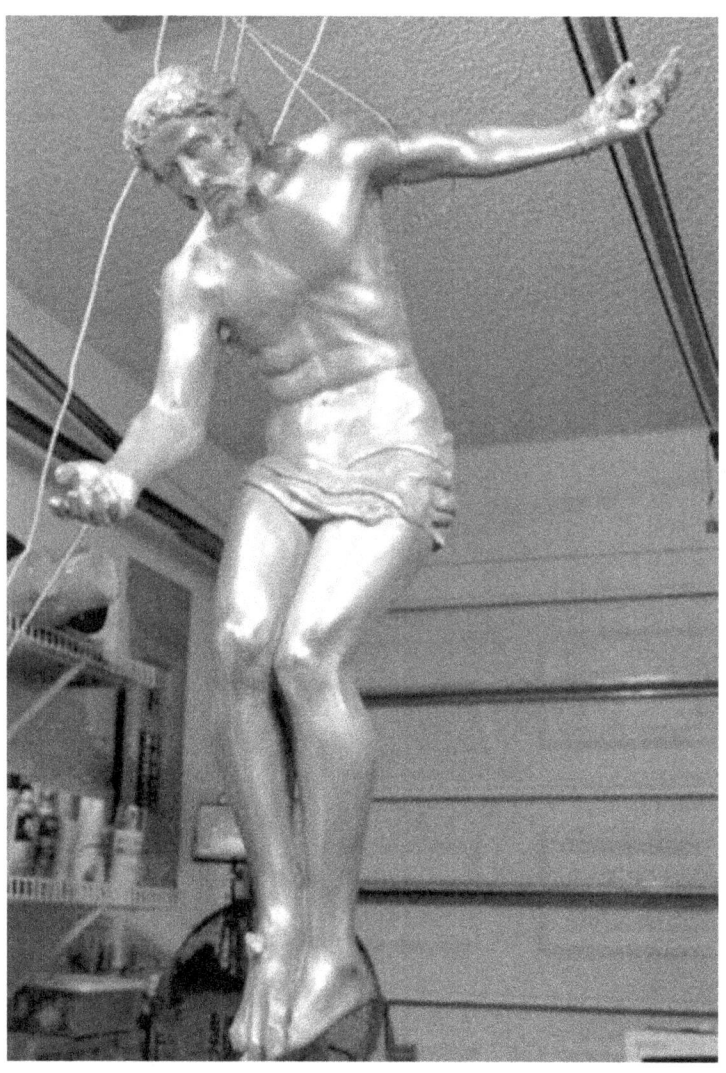

*"I know I have missed Him in many of those ten thousand places,
But I also know that He was always there.
And now, at last, I know
it should always have been about
Him."*

Father Harold Buckley

Appendix

FIRST LINE INDEX

FIRST LINE INDEX	TITLE	PAGE
A baleful pail full of pleading tears	Is the Light Always Warm	101
a crackling flame of flowers	Autumn	95
Again, I hear her moaning in the night	Again, I Hear Her Moaning	4
All love…all *life* is incomplete.	Walking in Silence	89
All time is past…..except For the moment we are in	A Certain Moment	167
Always the wide eyed boy	There Are Places Where…	76
And of a sudden, even at my look	Sudden	84
Anne, at the edge of terror	At the Suicide of Anne Sexton	18
Are brooks ever really too broad for leaping	Brooks and Leaping	174
Are you so sure that lilacs listen?	Skies	86
as white imprisoned all color, and snow	Fearful Notes	105
be tender or be mute	Talisman	17
Before the dawn draws back the night's Soft sable	When Morning Comes	120
Between the razor-sleek slicing of the dark	Crossing on the Ferry	107
Blessed Is the Child with withered cheeks	The Child with the Ancient Face	14
blind as the rain, death walks without eyes.	Blind as the Rain	118
Brighter Than Bird Song	Is He	121
carrying stones to crooked walls	New England	103
Clay is kinder to my hands…and heart	After Dress-Rehearsal of the "Caine"	70
confusing: that a single strand of silk	A Web	97
Darkness is the silence of the eye	Silence	148
Day-done and dark As the last spark	Day-done and Dark	190
Death and dreams, Dreams and death	Death and Dreams	166
Death has a stench	Why We Like Flowers	109
Do not see only Jesus in my eyes	Moistened Clay	158
Do we contain in this moment everything we are?	Dryness and Tears	181
events forever fall on us	Events	196
God, who is love	Transfiguration	127
Good Morning, I said to God	"Good Morning," I said to God	123
hate has fallen like a tree	LONDON/DERRY	77
He had just come into the city	The Centurion	212
He had that look, the empty, lonely	A Death in Iraq	29
He stands in the wild synagogue of the sensuous	The Sensuous Rose	112
He was a child, Shining-eyed and wide with wonder	Outside my window…	22
here along the rim	Here Along the Rim	184

APPENDIX

His weight upon the waves	Judas	219
How much of laughter is really crying?	Questions 101	160
How shall I say?	The Gift	129
I am Bartimaeus and I am blind	Bartimaeus	222
I am not the face looking back at me	Mirror	173
I did not *know* thy name Before the willows bent	Pain Has No Name	66
I do not love (yet would not be without)	The Artist	195
I don't remember Time, with such a kindness, spent	Past Regained	67
I had not seen this death in me	Seeming Death	164
I have watched so many leaves go sere and dry	September	83
I heard through the words, I saw	LoveatLast	194
I loved them all. And told "forevers' without a lie	Poverty	65
I never met the man whose death I mourn	I Never Met the Man	73
I remember the blossoms.	The Park Bench	192
I see the old fig tree winter-wrapped	Winter-Wakening	87
I stood there, my shoulder against the years,	Light Without Shadow	151
I was in light, not water	Cape Cod	94
I was listening for the sounds that hide in the light	Now, The Light	193
I was standing in those dim eighty years	To My God of Silence	152
I went at mid-morning round the house	The Hawk	82
I went once like an island people	More Than a Dream	135
I will always walk quite near you in the light	A Shadow Speaks	108
If I had known their richness and their wonder	"80"	149
If I said that "love was actually loneliness"	Love is Loneliness	55
if I set my heart on hearts alone	If I Had Set My Heart	49
In the morning my eyes So slowly	Morning…	153
In those first steps with open heart you walked	To an unloved child	69
is it enough to be sorry?	On Reading About the Death	7
Is the hand withheld, less guilty	Innocence	159
Is there one name that sums up all your life?	The Name	122
It inches, this untiring, lunar-tilting sea	The Gulls	102
It is that time. The landscape is resigned	To a Rose in October	90
it was a moment by a mirror	Reflection	142
It was around mid-day	Among the Palms	154
It was June. Some men, with sand on their elbows	Other Places	32
It was my great pain That being small I still knew	Pebbles	187
It was toward evening	John The Baptist	225
It wasn't as though the sky was	THE MAGI: A JOURNEY	130
Kind King, O Jesus joy, and fire of friends	HOLY WEEK	124
Last night it was while veiled in censer smoke	Last Night	125
Life is such a thing of hope	Silent Cay	168
Like little children, we climb up on to the knee	A Child's Tale	57
Long before the stars, great capless jars	A Soul Speaks	140
Looking out the window of the train	Tombstones	177
Lord, I hear	Rosary After Mass	128
Love is not a desert	The Green Wood	52

Memory is the only faculty that can defeat Time	Time's Defeat	44
Mother, your ministers have made	After Gertrud von le Fort	180
Must I everywhere behold my "roots"	Meaning?	170
My prismed lady; a watery cast	My Mother	47
My road seems wrong against the night	Standing in a Night's Snow	88
Night had nailed her darkness to the main mast	Hope	169
No one heard the pressing-God against our sky	The Annunciation:	120
nothing knows what fingers know	After Peter's Class	189
Often in good-nights Lovers sway in place	Often in Good Nights	39
Old Lear in a court	Old Lear	53
Old Simeon had reached an age	Old Simeon	218
Once I too was great, And changed the course	Vermont	85
Once, I ached, each morning, like a millstone for grist	Aching	147
Our prayers impregnate the possible	What We Dream	119
While Pilates useless gesture	Simon of Cyrene	209
Prometheus is weeping by a rock in Hiroshima	August, 1945	28
Righteousness had killed Him	Good Friday	134
Scoffed, cartooned, and caricatured	The Alchemists:	143
She had heard about the paralytic	Mary Magdalene	200
Silence is the mind's air and spring	Silence	162
Silence sits in the dark Waiting for my eyes	Darkness	145
So much pain and emptiness Have shaped words	Emptiness and song	140
Some place in this impassive stone	Impassive Stone	92
Some place in this leering night	Of Dust and Dreams	63
some years, even some loves, somehow	On the Port Jefferson Ferry	172
Staring at the ground	Summer Emptiness	197
superior minds and great hearts, without faith	Without Faith	64
Tears cannot unstop the silence made by shrapnel	Prayer for a boy I taught	27
Tears, like painful prisms	Tears	170
that first time round, how much of joy there was	english III	178
that little bit of bloodied ear drowned out your palette	To Vincent	186
That pulse, dear heart, that binds	Love's Fierce File	51
that shape of sound lipped and tongue-curved	A Word	188
The barn loomed octagonal and black	The Barn Loomed	93
The Coffee was still warm.	A Father	46
The dark-lake cry of the loon	A Night Cry	90
The heart never knew that its sweet song	Old But Not Forgetful	42
The little juggler had only baubles to toss	Le Jongleur de Notre Dame	191
The part that breathes in me	When They Meet	179
the snow began disguised as mist	The First Fall	104
The sound *beneath* the sound is what I long to hear	Songs I've Heard	139
The years: When I heard the music	My Father	183
Then loomed the louring of that night	After Night…	116
There is a certain sadness sometimes seen	A Certain Sadness	20
this sound of summer bursting like the philharmonic	The Sound of Summer	91
Though I had seen the wall, and heard some call	The Garden Wall	41

APPENDIX

though I have never held so sweet a holding		Celibacy	40
Though love be the dupe of Time		Love's Time	45
Through the lattice-bend of boughs		The Catskills	100
Time, after all, has little hands		The Lock of Love	43
Today I walked a country filled with snow		Walking in the Snow	175
Waves came in like angry cockatoos		Freedom	34
We are locked in what is *not*		M.I.A.	33
we had taken the willow path		The Wounded Thrush	79
We have walked with wildness		Nature's Gift	106
We see them each night: Faces lopped of life		The Pain of Honor	31
We waited, But no one came.		Soldier	35
We were rowing on Galilee		Peter on the Lake	220
We will count the times, And seek the times		Count The Times	68
Wet as willow-white		Renewal	117
What does the black-eyed susan see?		Inklings	171
What hand will I hold		Courage	78
What will stop when you stop laughing?		What Will Stop	75
What?! After he takes my cloak		A Clown Christ	8
When all the grieving and congregating hearts		For Some Children at Play	72
When I was a child The crushing		Feeling	71
When Peter sat among his friends		St. Peter	113
Where once I feared the unseen force of time's		Unfeeling Time	74
While a phono thundered the beat		Unlatched and Waiting	48
With stars and planets vying for the gift		November Night at North Sea	98
With still some wild wonder where tears		An Old Man at the Catholic Worker	12
With your tiny single-fingered hands impale the Time		When Quiet comes	144
Won't you, my dear, Come over here.		Won't you, my Dear	156
Wounded hearts had waited while the fat		How Cider Lasts	150
Yes, there are Heathcliffs, who, like old Lear		After Wuthering Heights	62
you are after all madam on the wrong side		The Wrong Side of the Sky	138
You breathe heavily And feel the pressure		To a young mother in a new age	16
you lock your faith with laser looks		8:30 Alchemy	114
You never left me where I would have to lean		To My Own Angel	115
You pick the locks of mystery with these so-little		"I do…"	50
You were brave		AT THE CATHOLIC WORKER	10
Your lovely touch that tended brooding care		On Your Seventieth Birthday	38

FR. BUCKLEY'S VOICE RECORDING

TITLE	PAGE
Again I Hear Her Moaning	4
A Certain Sadness	20
Prayer for a boy I taught	27
A Death in Iraq	29
The Pain of Honor	31
The Garden Wall	41
My Mother	47
I Never Met The Man	73
London/Derry	77
The Wounded Thrush	79
The Hawk	82
Sudden	84
Standing in the Night's Snow	88
Impassive Stone	92
Autumn	95
New England	103
The Sensuous Rose	112
St. Peter	113
Renewal	117
The Name	122
Last Night	125
The Annunciation	126
The Magi: A Journey	130
Won't You My Dear	156
Walking in the Snow	175
Events	196
Simon of Cyrene	209

www.ingramcontent.com/pod-product-compliance
Lightning Source LLC
Chambersburg PA
CBHW081454040426
42446CB00016B/3238